THE REVOLUTIONARY WAR

A SOURCEBOOK ON COLONIAL AMERICA

THE REVOLUTIONARY WAR

A SOURCEBOOK ON COLONIAL AMERICA

Edited by Carter Smith

AMERICAN ALBUMS FROM THE COLLECTIONS OF
THE LIBRARY OF CONGRESS

THE MILLBROOK PRESS, *Brookfield, Connecticut*

Cover: The surrender of the British troops at Yorktown, a hand-colored French engraving by Mondhare, 1781.

Title Page: Boston, under siege, being evacuated by British troops and American loyalists, a contemporary German woodcut.

Contents Page: American flags and artillery in an army camp, a steel engraving, nineteenth century.

Back Cover: Combat between John Paul Jones's Bonhomme Richard *and Richard Peausch's* Serapis, *a hand-colored engraving after a drawing by Richard Paten, 1781.*

Library of Congress Cataloging-in-Publication Data

The Revolutionary War: a Sourcebook on Colonial America / edited by
Carter Smith.
     p. cm -- (American Albums from the Collections of the Library of
Congress)
    Includes bibliographical references and index.
    Summary: Describes and illustrates the historical, political, military,
social, and cultural aspects of the Revolutionary War through a variety
of images created during that period.
    ISBN 1-56294-039-2 (lib. bdg.) ISBN 1-878841-69-6 (pbk.)
    1. United States--History--Revolution, 1775-1783--Juvenile litera-
ture. 2. United States--History--Revolution, 1775-1783--Pictorial works
--Juvenile literature. 3. United States--History--Revolution, 1775-1783
Sources--Juvenile literature. [1. United States--History--Revolution,
1775-1783--Sources.] I. Smith, C. Carter II. Series.
E208.R48 1991
                                91-13938
                                CIP
                                AC

 Created in association with Media Projects Incorporated

C. Carter Smith, *Executive Editor*
Lelia Wardwell, *Managing Editor*
Charles A. Wills, *Consulting Editor*
Kimberly Horstman, *Researcher*
Lydia Link, *Designer*
Athena Angelos, *Photo Researcher*

The consultation of Bernard F. Reilly, Jr., Head Curator of the
Prints and Photographs Division of the Library of Congress, is
gratefully acknowledged.

Contents

DECLARATION OF INDEPENDENCE WITH THE TREATY OF ALLIANCE BETWEEN HIS MOST CHRISTIAN MAJESTY AND THE UNITED STATES OF AMERICA

NEW WINDSOR

PROTECTION TO REBELS ON SUBMISSION

BILL TO PARDON THE REBELS

CONCILIATORY BILLS LETTERS AND PROCLAMATIONS FROM THE BRITISH COMMISSIONERS

NORTH AMERICA

Introduction

THE REVOLUTIONARY WAR is one of the initial volumes in a series published by the Millbrook Press titled AMERICAN ALBUMS FROM THE COLLECTIONS OF THE LIBRARY OF CONGRESS, and one of six books in the series subtitled SOURCEBOOKS ON COLONIAL AMERICA. They treat the early history of our homeland from its discovery and early settlement through the colonial and revolutionary wars and the establishment of the United States in the late eighteenth century.

The editor's basic goal for the series is to make available to the student many of the original visual documents—the early maps, prints, drawings, engravings, broadsides—preserved in the Library of Congress as records of the American past. An attempt has been made to rely as heavily as possible on works contemporaneous with the events and persons portrayed. This affords the student contact with the primary materials used by historians, and provides a window on that early world. Some late images, either creative reconstructions of earlier events or renderings of the sites of history as they survived in the nineteenth century, provide a look back at the colonial period from a closer vantage point than the twentieth century. In some cases these later works present a more heroic, Eurocentric picture of American history than that to which we would subscribe today, but in most cases the images provide the only authentic records of the now-vanished buildings and towns of early America.

Each of these visual sourcebooks also includes, in addition to images, one or more illustrated timelines, providing a capsulated chronology of the main political, military, cultural, and economic events of the period.

THE REVOLUTIONARY WAR reproduces many of the prints, broadsides, maps, and other original works preserved in the Library of Congress special collections divisions, and a few from its general book collections. The majority of items in this volume are from the rich holdings of early printing and engraving in the Library's Rare Book and Special Collections Division and Prints and Photographs Division.

The Library has one of the major archives of colonial American printing from the Revolutionary period. This includes thousands of pamphlets, broadsides and newspapers of the time. While produced and circulated at a rate far slower (and an expense far greater) than the "street literature" of today, these publications were the principle vehicles of political information and debate in the colonies. These broadsides, pamphlets, and newspapers are invaluable documents of the political debate and issues which impelled the colonists toward revolution and, ultimately, independence.

In contrast to the pamphlets and newspapers, few prints were produced in the colonies themselves. John Thackara's small engraving of the State House in Philadelphia is one of the few American view prints from the time. The portrait of George Washington by Noel Le Mire (after a painting by Jean Baptiste Le Paon) and François Godefroy's masterly engraving of the Battle of Lexington were produced in France, where the art of engraving was well established. These and other works indicate the level of interest (and sympathy) in much of the Old World for the American revolt. France eagerly aided American opposition to its old colonial rival in the Western Hemisphere.

For other images of the period we resort to nineteenth-century portrayals produced by the first generation of American illustrators, such as Alonzo Chappel, F.O.C. Darley, and Benson Lossing. These citizens of a country just old enough to have a proper history began reconstruction of the American past.

The pictoral documents included here represent a small but telling portion of the rich record of the American past that the Library of Congress preserves in its role as the national library.

BERNARD F. REILLY, JR

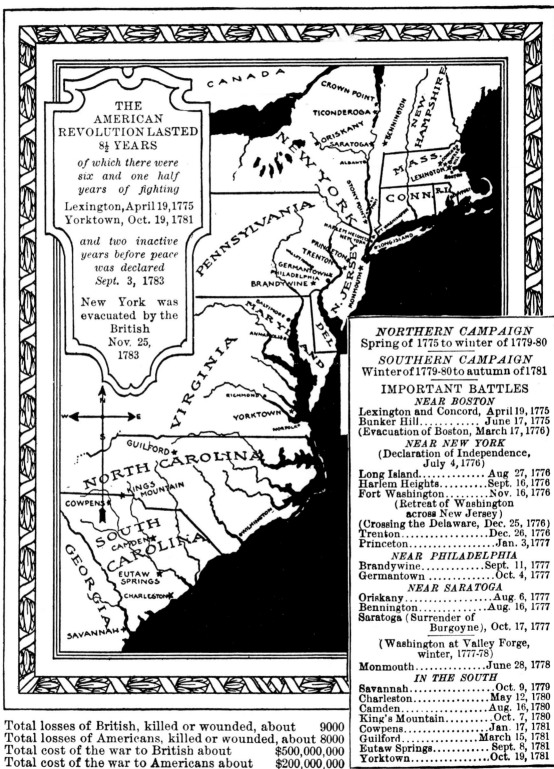

THE AMERICAN REVOLUTION LASTED 8½ YEARS

of which there were six and one half years of fighting

Lexington, April 19, 1775
Yorktown, Oct. 19, 1781

and two inactive years before peace was declared Sept. 3, 1783

New York was evacuated by the British Nov. 25, 1783

NORTHERN CAMPAIGN
Spring of 1775 to winter of 1779-80

SOUTHERN CAMPAIGN
Winter of 1779-80 to autumn of 1781

IMPORTANT BATTLES
NEAR BOSTON
Lexington and Concord, April 19, 1775
Bunker Hill............June 17, 1775
(Evacuation of Boston, March 17, 1776)
NEAR NEW YORK
(Declaration of Independence, July 4, 1776)
Long Island..............Aug 27, 1776
Harlem Heights.........Sept. 16, 1776
Fort Washington........Nov. 16, 1776
(Retreat of Washington across New Jersey)
(Crossing the Delaware, Dec. 25, 1776)
Trenton..................Dec. 26, 1776
Princeton.................Jan. 3, 1777
NEAR PHILADELPHIA
Brandywine.............Sept. 11, 1777
Germantown ....Oct. 4, 1777
NEAR SARATOGA
Oriskany..................Aug. 6, 1777
Bennington.............Aug. 16, 1777
Saratoga (Surrender of Burgoyne), Oct. 17, 1777
(Washington at Valley Forge, winter, 1777-78)
Monmouth..............June 28, 1778
IN THE SOUTH
Savannah..................Oct. 9, 1779
Charleston...............May 12, 1780
Camden...................Aug. 16, 1780
King's Mountain..........Oct. 7, 1780
Cowpens.................Jan. 17, 1781
Guilford.................March 15, 1781
Eutaw Springs............Sept. 8, 1781
Yorktown.................Oct. 19, 1781

Total losses of British, killed or wounded, about   9000
Total losses of Americans, killed or wounded, about 8000
Total cost of the war to British about $500,000,000
Total cost of the war to Americans about $200,000,000

The Revolutionary War

The first shots of the Revolutionary War were fired at Lexington and Concord, Massachusetts, in April 1775. The early battles of the war—Bunker Hill and the siege of Boston, the capture of Fort Ticonderoga—were fought in the Northern colonies. In late 1775 and 1776, the war spread to the north and south. Patriot forces unsuccessfully invaded Canada, while a British invasion of the southern colonies was also unsuccessful.

After the British left Boston, the focus of the fighting shifted to the middle colonies. George Washington's Continental Army was driven out of New York in the summer and fall of 1776. Washington retreated across New Jersey, but scored victories in Trenton and Princeton during the winter of 1776-1777.

The summer of 1777 saw a major British defeat in the Saratoga campaign, which included battles in New York and Vermont. However, British successes at Brandywine Creek and Germantown, Pennsylvania, led to the capture of Philadelphia, and the Continental Army spent a bitter winter at Valley Forge. After Valley Forge, Washington turned north, fought the inconclusive battle of Monmouth Court House in June 1778, and moved the Continental Army to positions around New York—where it remained for three years.

In 1779, the war shifted to the Southern colonies. The British won control of much of the region after a string of victories including the capture of Savannah, Georgia, in October 1779 and Charleston, South Carolina, in May, 1780. However, local patriots and Continental Army units began striking back, winning battles in North and South Carolina in 1780 and 1781. In the summer of 1781, Washington led the Continental Army south, aided by French troops and warships. After a brief siege, a British Army surrendered at Yorktown, Virginia, on October 19, 1781—the last major battle of the conflict.

COMMON SENSE;

ADDRESSED TO THE

INHABITANTS

OF

AMERICA,

On the following interesting

SUBJECTS.

I. Of the Origin and Design of Government in general, with concise Remarks on the English Constitution.

II. Of Monarchy and Hereditary Succession.

III. Thoughts on the present State of American Affairs.

IV. Of the present Ability of America, with some miscellaneous Reflections.

Man knows no Master save creaing HEAVEN,
Or those whom choice and common good ordain.

THOMSON.

PHILADELPHIA;
Printed, and Sold, by R. BELL, in Third-Street.
MDCCLXXVI.

Part I: April 1775-June 1776
The Fight for a New Nation Begins

Thomas Paine's Common Sense *circulated widely in the colonies; by June 1776, more than a hundred thousand copies had been sold. Paine condemned Britain, calling King George III a "royal brute." His arguments for self-government influenced the Declaration of Independence.*

Tensions between British troops and the citizens in and around Boston reached such a high point by April 1775 that armed conflict broke out. The British army had about four thousand troops in the area, who were organized and well equipped compared to the colonists. Opposing the British were the Minutemen—the first Americans to fight for independence. These volunteers played an important role in the early part of the war. Their skill and determination surprised the British army at the battles of Lexington and Concord. The British were even more surprised to find themselves under siege in Boston, as the colonial army grew in strength and numbers around them.

Nevertheless, the leaders of the Revolution realized they needed to organize a professional army in order to fight the British. Three weeks into the war, the Second Continental Congress gathered in Philadelphia. The delegates laid down the plans for the Continental Army and appointed George Washington as its commander in chief.

At the beginning of the war, many colonists still did not want complete independence from Britain. But as, their distrust of Parliament and King George III grew during the first year of the war, the desire for independence increased. In January 1776, a writer named Thomas Paine published a pamphlet entitled *Common Sense*. This document argued for complete independence from Britain and boldly attacked not only King George but the idea of monarchy itself. Many colonists either read *Common Sense* or heard about it, and Paine's stirring words inspired a large number of people to join the Patriot cause.

April 1, 1775 **June 22, 1775**

WORLD HISTORY

Edmund Burke

Lord North

1775 British statesman Edmund Burke urges Parliament to compromise with the colonies; he is unsuccessful.

1775 French dramatist Caron de Beaumarchais writes the *Barber of Seville*; it is later adapted into an opera by Italian composer Gioacchino Rossini.

April Austria acquires Delagoa Bay, an important harbor for trade on the southeast coast of Africa.
•Empress Maria Theresa abolishes the law forcing tenants to work for landlords for certain days a year in Bohemia and in the Austrian states.

1775 James Bruce returns to Britain after exploring Ethiopia and the Blue Nile in North Africa.

1775 Bread shortages and a poor harvest cause violent riots in parts of France. This so-called "flour war" causes problems for the French government's reform policies.

1775 Peter Boehler, a bishop of the Moravian Church in Germany, dies. Boehler left his native Germany to minister the black slaves in Savannah, Georgia.

COLONIAL HISTORY THE REVOLUTIONARY WAR

April 1 Daniel Boone establishes the settlement of Boonesborough in what will become Kentucky.

April 14 Benjamin Franklin and Dr. Benjamin Rush organize the first formal movement in the colonies against slavery by founding the Abolition Society for the Relief of Free Negroes Unlawfully Held in Bondage.

April 18 Paul Revere, William Dawes, and Dr. Samuel Prescott alert the Massachusetts countryside to the British advance on Lexington. John Hancock and Samuel Adams escape Lexington before the British attack.

April 19 At the Battles of Lexington and Concord, the British clash with Patriot Minutemen, marking the beginning of the Revolutionary War.

The Minutemen of the Revolution

May 10 Ethan Allen, Benedict Arnold, and the Green Mountain Boys seize Fort Ticonderoga on Lake Champlain.
•The Second Continental Congress meets in Philadelphia. John Hancock is elected president of the Congress.

May 16 The first constitution in America to be tested by popular vote is completed in Massachusetts. It was later rejected. An acceptable constitution was finally passed on June 7, 1778.

May 20 The Mecklenburg Declaration of Independence is proclaimed at Charlotte, North Carolina, although its authenticity has never been proved.

1775 The British begin to hire German mercenaries (commonly called Hessians) for service in America.

1775 Attempts by Britain to hire Russian and Dutch troops to fight in America are unsuccessful.

1775 The first two parts of *M'Fingal*, a satire on American Tories by John Trumbull, are published.

1775 Philip Freneau, "the poet of the American Revolution," publishes patriotic pamphlets.

June 15 George Washington is appointed to lead the Continental Army by Congress.

June 17 The Battle of Bunker Hill (actually fought on nearby Breed's Hill) takes place outside of Boston.
•Congress appoints four major generals for the Continental Army—Charles Lee, Israel Putnam, Philip Schuyler, and Artemas Ward.

June 22 To raise funds for the Patriot cause, Congress issues paper money.

George III

August 23 King George III rejects Congress's Olive Branch Petition for peace.

1775 Pope Pius VI (Giovanni Angelico Braschi) is elected to the papacy; he serves until his death in 1817.

November 1775 Philosopher and writer Johann Wolfgang von Goethe, whose novels are popular with the colonists, arrives at Weimar in Germany.

1775 Catherine II of Russia reorganizes local governments, assuring the people freedom of trade and industry.

1775 Alessandro Volta, an Italian scientist, begins a series of experiments which eventually leads to the invention of the electric storage battery.

1775 In Germany, especially in Hesse-Cassel, 29,000 men are pressed into service by their local rulers to fight for the British in America.

1775 War between Britain and the Marathas empire in southwest India begins.

1775 The Shah of Persia (modern-day Iran) captures Basra in what is now Iraq.

1775 Britain takes over the India-China opium trade from Portugal.

July 3 George Washington assumes command of the Continental Army (about 14,000 men) in Cambridge, Massachusetts.

George Washington

July 5 Congress sends the Olive Branch Petition, expressing hopes for peace, to King George III; it is rejected.

July 25 Dr. Benjamin Church is appointed first surgeon general of the Continental Army.

July 26 Congress establishes the Post Office with Benjamin Franklin as Postmaster General.

August 1 Thomas Paine publishes an article on women's rights in the *Pennsylvania Gazette*.

October 4 Dr. Benjamin Church, the first surgeon general, is accused of and court-martialed for "criminal correspondence with the enemy."

October 13 A South Carolina delegate to the Continental Congress attempts, unsuccessfully, to discharge blacks from the Continental Army.

October 18 British forces burn Falmouth (present-day Portland), Maine.

November 7 Lord Dunmore, British governor of Virginia, establishes martial law and recruits local Loyalists into the British Army. He also offers freedom to slaves who join the Loyalist forces.

November 10 Two battalions of Marines are organized by Congress as part of the Continental Navy.

November 13 A Patriot force led by General Richard Montgomery occupies Montreal, Canada.

November 29 Congress appoints a Committee of Secret Correspondence to seek aid from friendly European nations.

December James Adair publishes a study of North American Indians and describes, among other things, the game of lacrosse played by the Cherokee Indians.

December 3 The first official American flag is raised on board the warship *Alfred*. Called the Congress Colors, it remains the American flag until the Stars and Stripes are adopted on June 14, 1777.

December 11 A force of Virginians and North Carolinians defeats Virginia Governor Lord Dunmore at Great Bridge, Virginia.

The first American flag

December 31 American forces led by Benedict Arnold and Richard Montgomery are driven back by the British in the Battle of Quebec.
•George Washington orders recruiting officers to allow free blacks to join the Continental Army.

A TIMELINE OF MAJOR EVENTS

PART I *April 1775-June 1776 The Fight for a New Nation Begins*

WORLD HISTORY

1776 British explorer James Cook makes his third voyage to the Pacific Ocean. On this expedition, he searches unsuccessfully along the northwest coast of North America for a passage to the Atlantic Ocean.

1776 British political reformer John Cartwright publishes "Take your Choice," a pamphlet arguing for reforms in the British Parliament. Cartwright advocated universal male suffrage and the abolition of slavery.

1776 Charles Burney, an important English music historian, publishes his four-volume *A General History of Music*. It will be become a classic, providing an in-depth study of the music and composers of the period.

1776 Portugal unifies its South American empire by forming the Viceroyalty of Rio de la Plata (Argentina, Bolivia, Paraguay, and Uruguay) in Rio de Janeiro.

James Watt's steam engine

1776 Adam Smith publishes *The Wealth of Nations,* a book which promotes the economic system that comes to be called capitalism.

1776 James Watt and Matthew Boulton produce their first commercial steam engine, which Watt designed in 1775, encouraging the Industrial Revolution in Britain.

COLONIAL HISTORY THE REVOLUTIONARY WAR

January 1 Virginia Governor Lord Dunmore orders the burning of Norfolk, Virginia.

January 5 New Hampshire adopts a state constitution, becoming the first colony to declare full independence from Britain.

January 9 Thomas Paine publishes *Common Sense*, a pamphlet which attacks King George III and argues

Thomas Paine

for colonial independence.

February 27 At the Battle of Moore's Creek Bridge, near Wilmington, Delaware, North Carolina Patriots defeat a band of Loyalists, ruining British plans for an invasion of the Wilmington-Cape Fear region.

February 28 Black poet and slave Phillis Wheatley is invited by George Washington to Cambridge because of a poem she wrote praising the general.

March 3 Congress appoints Silas Deane as colonial agent to France to secure financial and military aid.

March 4-5 American forces capture Dorchester Heights overlooking Boston Harbor. This allows the Americans to place cannons brought from Fort

British ships in Boston Harbor

Ticonderoga by Henry Knox in range of the British in Boston.

March 7-17 The British, led by General William Howe, evacuate Boston.

March 14 Congress recommends a policy for disarming all Loyalists.

April 6 Congress proclaims American ports open to all nations except Great Britain.

April 12 The North Carolina Provincial Assembly is the first to send delegates to Congress and instructs them to support independence from Britain.

April 13 After the evacu-

ation of Boston, George Washington leads the Continental Army to New York City.

May 2 The French government, through secret agent Caron de Beaumarchais, sends $1 million worth of arms to America.

May 3 British forces led by General Charles Cornwallis join General Clinton's forces off the coast of the Carolinas.

May 9-16 A Continental Navy force, led by Commodore Esek Hopkins, raids the British colony of Nassau in the Bahamas, capturing large amounts of munitions.

General Charles Cornwallis

1776 German dramatist, Friedrich von Klinger, writes *Sturm und Drang*, an emotional play which later gives the literary movement Sturm und Drang (Storm and Stress) its name.

1776 Scottish philosopher David Hume dies.

1776 Amedeo Avogadro, an Italian physicist and philosopher, is born. Known primarily in chemistry for his *Avogadro's Law*, he is one of the founders of physical chemistry and coined the term "molecule."

1776 Russian field marshal Grigori Potemkin, favorite of Czarina Catherine, organizes his nation's Black Sea naval fleet.

1776 English philosopher Jeremy Bentham publishes his first book, *Fragment on Government*, a criticism of the English legal system.

1776 The Bolshoi Ballet becomes state supported in Moscow.

1776 In Naples, chief minister Bernardo Tannucci, who has been legal advisor to the crown for twenty years, is forced to retire. (Tannucci reformed the brutal laws of the Neapolitan Legal Code and restricted the privileges of the nobility.)

David Hume

May 10 Congress authorizes each of the thirteen colonies to form new state governments.

May 15 The Virginia delegation to Congress is authorized to support independence by its state government.

Charles Lee

June A British fleet led by General William Howe and Admiral Richard Howe arrives in New York City.

June 4 American General Charles Lee arrives from New York to defend Charleston, South Carolina.

June 7 Virginia delegate Richard Henry Lee

The Declaration of Independence Committee

offers a formal resolution calling for independence.

June 11 Congress appoints John Adams, Benjamin Franklin, Thomas Jefferson, Roger Sherman, and Robert Livingston to draft a declaration of independence based on Lee's resolution. The committee elects Thomas Jefferson to write the document.

June 12 Congress appoints a committee led by John Dickinson to prepare a draft of the Articles of Confederation.
•The Virginia Assembly passes the first state bill of rights, drafted by George Mason, as part of the Virginia Constitution.

June 27 Colonial traitor Thomas Hickey is publicly hanged in New York for conspiring to hand George Washington over to the British.

June 28 With a few changes by John Adams and Benjamin Franklin, Jefferson's draft of the Declaration of Independence is presented to Congress.
•General Charles Lee successfully defends Fort Moultrie at Charleston, South Carolina, against British forces.

July 2 Most members of the Continental Congress vote to support Lee's resolution for independence.

The British in New York City

THE WAR BEGINS: THE BATTLE OF LEXINGTON

America's war for independence began on April 19, 1775, in the town of Lexington, Massachusetts. Colonists had gathered a large supply of weapons and arms in nearby Concord. On the night of April 18, British General Thomas Gage sent seven hundred soldiers to destroy the supplies and capture two revolutionary leaders, Samuel Adams and John Hancock. Three Boston citizens, Paul Revere, William Dawes, and Dr. Samuel Prescott, learned of the maneuver and rode through the area, warning of the British advance. After hearing the news, Patriots across the countryside grabbed their muskets and rushed to Lexington. These volunteers were known as the Minutemen because they pledged to be ready for battle at a minute's notice.

When the British reached Lexington at dawn, seventy Minutemen were waiting for them on the village green. After the rebels refused Major John Pitcairn's order to lay down their weapons, the first shot was fired—but no one knows if it came from a British or Patriot musket. In the brief battle that followed, eight Americans were killed and nine were wounded. The remaining Minutemen scattered while the British soldiers, called "Redcoats" because of their red uniforms, marched on to Concord.

In *Provincial Congress,*

Cambridge, February 14, 1775.

WHEREAS it appeared necessary for the Defence of the Lives, Liberties, and Properties of the Inhabitants of this Province, that this Congress on the first Day of their next Session, should be made fully acquainted with the Number and Military Equipments of the Militia, and Minute Men in this Province; and also the Town Stock of Ammunition in each Town and District:—

It is therefore RESOLVED, That it be and it is hereby recommended, to the commanding Officers of each Regiment of Minute Men, that now is or shall be formed in this Province, that they review the several Companies in their respective Regiments, or cause them to be reviewed, and take an exact State of their Numbers, and Equipment, —and where there is any Company that is not incorporated into a Regiment, the commanding Officer thereof shall review the several Companies, or cause them to be reviewed, and take a like State of their Numbers and Equipment.—And it is also recommended to the Colonels or commanding Officers of each Regiment of Militia in this Province, that they review the several Companies in their respective Regiments, or cause them to be reviewed, and take a State of their Numbers and Accoutrements; which said State of the Minute Men and Militia, shall be by said Officers returned in Writing to this Congress, on the first Day of their Session after the Adjournment.——

And it is further RESOLVED, That it be recommended to the Select-Men of each Town and District in the Province, that on the same Day they make return in Writing of the State of the Town and District Stock of Ammunition, and War-like Stores to this Congress.

Signed by Order of the Provincial Congress,

JOHN HANCOCK, President.

A true Extract from the Minutes,

BENJAMIN LINCOLN, Secretary.

Because of increasing tensions between colonists and British troops in the winter of 1774-75, the rebels began organizing their own fighting force. This document (above), requests information about the number of Minutemen in the Massachusetts Bay area, and asks them to report to their commanding officers. John Hancock, one of the leaders of the Patriot cause, signed this resolution in February 1775.

"Disperse, ye rebels!" commanded Major John Pitcairn when he met the colonial Minutemen on the Lexington green. When they refused, the first shot of the Revolutionary War rang out. The battle is shown in this 1775 print (opposite page, top).

To put down revolutionary activities, General Thomas Gage kept a large force of Redcoats in the city of Boston. As this 1775 map (below) shows, three major hills, Roxbury Hill, Water Town Hill, and Winter Hill, surrounded the city. These hills became ideal places for the Patriot armies to set up their camps. In the upper left-hand corner, British soldiers are returning from the battles of Lexington and Concord.

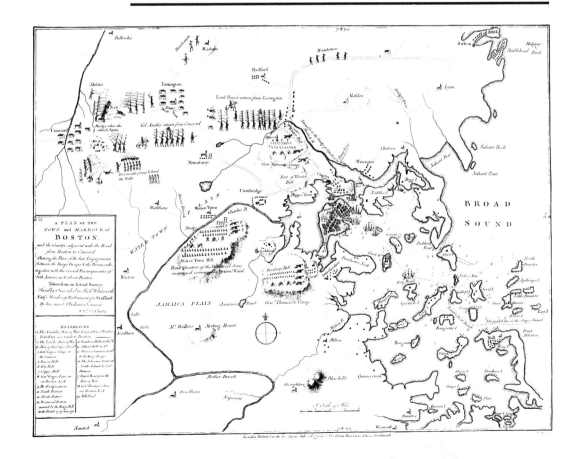

THE BATTLE OF CONCORD

After leaving the Americans to count their dead and wounded at Lexington, the Redcoats marched on to Concord. There they destroyed part of the colonists' supply of arms and gunpowder and headed back to Boston. A group of Minutemen fired at the Redcoats at the Old North Bridge. The British fought off the attack, though they lost three men, and continued on to Boston. As more farmers and townspeople from the area heard about the fighting, they took up their muskets and attacked the retreating British from behind trees and stone fences. Despite the fire, the British soldiers continued marching the sixteen miles to Boston. By evening the British had retreated to the safety of their camp, just barely escaping a force of Minutemen sent from Salem and Marblehead to block them. The Patriots then closed in around Boston, beginning a siege that would last almost a year. The British had lost 73 men and 174 more were wounded in the day's fighting. The Americans had fared better: only 49 men were killed and 41 were wounded.

The British army retreated from Concord down the main road. In this engraving (above), based on a painting by Alonzo Chappel, the Redcoats are being harassed by irregular groups of militia.

Shortly after the fighting at Lexington and Concord, this broadside (right) was published in Salem. The column at the far right lists the names of forty colonists who were killed and twenty who were wounded. Several features of this poster indicate the printer's efforts to stir up public feeling in favor of the Patriots and against the British, including the strong language in the headline and the report, the coffins, and the elegies to the dead.

THE AMERICANS CAPTURE FORT TICONDEROGA

The Green Mountain Boys were a regiment made up of settlers who lived west of the Green Mountains. Since 1770 they had been defending their claim to land in Vermont, which had not yet become a colony of its own and had staged many successful attacks against land agents and British officials from New York.

In May 1775, Ethan Allen led his Green Mountain Boys north to Lake Champlain, on the New York-Vermont border. Allen brought his men to Hand's Cove, two miles south of Fort Ticonderoga, where he joined forces with Benedict Arnold, another Patriot officer. The Americans stormed the fort at dawn, surprising the sleeping British troops. Two days later, the Americans captured Crown Point, another British stronghold. The Americans now controlled all of Lake Champlain. No lives were lost on either side in these attacks. The Continental Congress awarded the Green Mountain Boys the same pay as Continental Army soldiers in honor of their victory.

Henry Knox (1750-1806; above) became the chief of artillery for the Continental Army, and he participated in every important battle of the Revolutionary War. At Ticonderoga he was responsible for seizing British arms and transporting them overland to Boston in the dead of winter—a remarkable feat.

Ticonderoga was abandoned after its capture. This view from the nineteenth century (below) shows the ruins of the fort as seen from Lake Champlain.

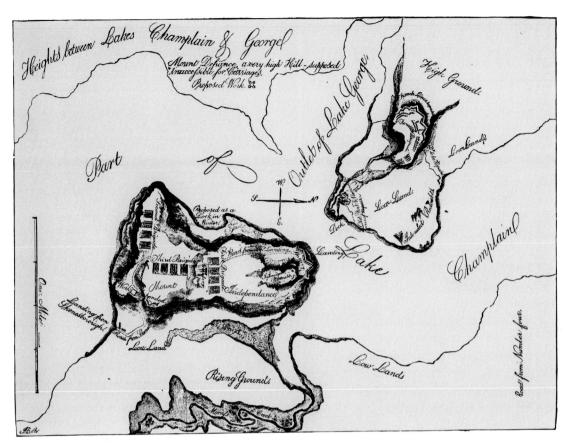

Located where Lake George and Lake Champlain meet at the Canadian border, Fort Ticonderoga occupied a strategic spot, as seen in this map (above). The fort was the scene of several major battles of the French and Indian War.

An important benefit of the American victory at Ticonderoga was the capture of British cannons. In the winter of 1775-1776, Henry Knox directed his men to take the artillery back to Boston, as shown in this illustration (right). These cannons were a major factor in forcing the British to evacuate Boston that summer.

THE BATTLE
OF BUNKER HILL

After the fighting at Lexington and Concord, a large force of Patriot soldiers held the British army under siege in Boston. The Patriots planned to obtain control of the hills surrounding the city in order to bombard the enemy forces below. Of the two hills on the Charlestown peninsula, Bunker Hill and Breed's Hill, the Americans chose Breed's Hill because it was closer to Boston.

On June 16, 1775, Colonel William Prescott led three American regiments up Breed's Hill. The British followed their commander, Thomas Gage in an attack to drive the Americans out. British warships bombarded the Americans from Boston Harbor while Redcoats, led by General William Howe, marched up the hillside. The Americans drove back two British attacks but, with ammunition running out, could not hold off a third. The struggle became known as the Battle of Bunker Hill, although this had little to do with the fighting. While the Americans lost Breed's Hill to the British, British forces suffered heavy losses. The courage of the defenders inspired Patriots throughout the colonies.

Thomas Gage (1721-87; this page, top) was commander in chief of British forces in North America at the start of the Revolutionary War. The Battle of Bunker Hill revealed his short-comings as a military leader, and in October 1775 he was recalled to England.

Joseph Warren (1741-75; this page, bottom) was a prominent Boston doctor and a strong supporter of the Revolution. Before the war broke out he had organized a Massachusetts militia and was elected major general. Warren is shown here preparing to lead his troops at the Battle of Bunker Hill.

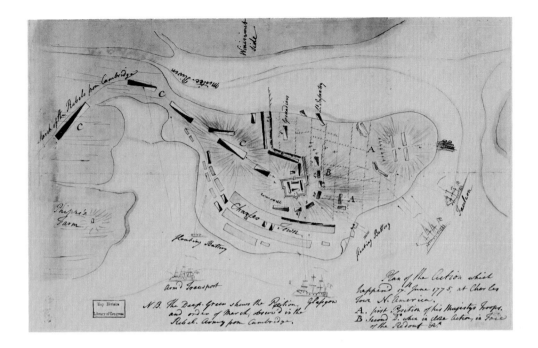

This map (above), drawn shortly after the battle, shows the advance of the British troops (labeled A and B) toward the American position (labeled C).

British warships fired shells from the harbor, causing much of Charlestown to catch fire, as shown in this engraving (below).

Addreſs to the Soldiers.

GENTLEMEN,

YOU are about to embark for *America*, to compel your Fellow Subjects there to ſubmit to POPERY and SLAVERY.

It is the Glory of the Britiſh Soldier, that he is the *Defender*, not the *Deſtroyer*, of the Civil and Religious Rights of the People. The *Engliſh* Soldiery are immortalized in Hiſtory, for their Attachment to the Religion and Liberties of their Country.

When King JAMES the Second endeavoured to introduce the Roman-catholic Religion and arbitrary Power into *Great Britain*, he had an Army encamped on *Hounſlow-Heath*, to terrify the People. Seven Biſhops were ſeized upon, and ſent to the Tower. But they appealed to the Laws of their Country, and were ſet at Liberty. When this News reached the Camp, the Shouts of Joy were ſo great, that they re-echoed in the Royal Palace. This, however, did not quite convince the King, of the Averſion of the Soldiers to be the Inſtruments of Oppreſſion againſt their Fellow Subjects. He therefore made another Trial. He ordered the Guards to be drawn up, and the Word was given, that thoſe who did not chuſe to ſupport the King's Meaſures, ſhould ground their Arms. When, behold, to his utter Confuſion, and their eternal Honour—the whole Body grounded their Arms!

You, Gentlemen, will ſoon have an Opportunity of ſhewing equal Virtue. You will be called upon to imbrue your Hands in the Blood of your Fellow Subjects in *America*, becauſe they will not admit to be Slaves, and are alarmed at the Eſtabliſhment of Popery and Arbitrary Power in one Half of their Country.

Whether you will draw thoſe Swords which have defended them againſt their Enemies, to butcher them into a Reſignation of their Rights, which they hold as the Sons of *Engliſhmen*, is in your Breaſts. That you will not ſtain the Laurels you have gained from *France*, by dipping them in Civil Blood, is every good Man's Hope.

Arts will no doubt be uſed to perſuade you, that it is your Duty to obey Orders; and that you are ſent upon the juſt and righteous Errand of cruſhing Rebellion But your own Hearts will tell you, that the People may be ſo ill treated, as to make Reſiſtance neceſſary. You know, that Violence and Injury offered from one Man to another, has always ſome Pretence of Right or Reaſon to juſtify it. So it is between the People and their Rulers.

Therefore, whatever hard Names and heavy Accuſations may be beſtowed upon your Fellow Subjects in *America*, be aſſured they have not deſerved them; but are driven, by the moſt cruel Treatment, into Deſpair, In this Deſpair they are compelled to defend their Liberties, after having tried, in Vain, every peaceable Means of obtaining Redreſs of their manifold Grievances.

Before God and Man they are right.

Your Honour then, Gentlemen, as Soldiers, and your Humanity as Men, forbid you to be the Inſtruments of forcing Chains upon your injured and oppreſſed Fellow Subjects. Remember that your firſt Obedience is due to God, and that whoever bids you ſhed innocent Blood, bids you act contrary to his Commandments.

—I am, GENTLEMEN,

your ſincere Well-wiſher,

AN OLD SOLDIER.

Americans tried to convince British soldiers to defy their officers' orders and join the revolutionary cause. This letter (left) to British troops on their way to America criticizes the policies of a king who would force his men to "shed innocent Blood." The letter appeared in a newspaper about the time of the Battle of Bunker Hill.

Joseph Warren was mortally wounded in the Battle of Bunker Hill, as shown in this engraving (opposite page, top) based on a painting by Alonzo Chappel. The British lost about a thousand men, while American dead and wounded totaled four hundred.

The Americans were finally forced to abandon their position on Breed's Hill after two hours of fierce fighting. News of their courage in holding off the British spread throughout the colonies and increased support for the revolution. Many young men came forward to enlist in the army. Citizens responded to broadsides such as this one (opposite page, bottom), which requests Patriots to donate supplies to the army.

TO all Gentlemen VOLUNTEERS, who prefer LIBERTY to SLAVERY, and are hearty Friends to the GRAND *AMERICAN* CAUSE; who are free and willing to ferve this STATE, in the Character of a Gentleman MATROSS, and learn the noble Art of Gunnery, in the Maffachufetts State Train of Artillery, commanded by Col. THOMAS CRAFTS, now ftationed in the Town and Harbour of *BOSTON*, and not to be removed but by Order of the honorable Houfe of Reprefentatives, or Council of faid State; let them appear at the Drum-Head, or at the ▓▓▓▓ ▓▓▓▓▓▓▓▓▓▓▓▓▓▓▓ where they fhall enter into prefent Pay ▓▓▓▓▓▓▓▓ ▓ *Eight Shillings per Month*. For their Encouragement they fhall receive *Twenty Dollars* Bounty on paffing Mufter, one Suit of Regimental Cloathes yearly, a Blanket, &c. with Arms and Accoutrements fuitable for a Gentleman Matrofs. For their further Encouragement, the Colonel would inform all Gentlemen Volunteers, that there are *twenty-two Non-commiffion Officers in each Company, who receive from three Pounds four and fix Pence, to three Pounds twelve per Month*; and as none will be accepted in faid Regiment, but Men of good Characters, fuch only will be promoted, whofe fteady Conduct and good Behaviour merits it.

☞ *You are defired to take Notice of the difference of Pay and Station.*

Golden Ball on Taunton Green

Thos Greenleaf Recruiting Officer

THE CONTINENTAL CONGRESS

The Continental Congress met for the second time on May 10, 1775, in Philadelphia. Most of the delegates had attended the first Congress, which had met the previous year, also in Philadelphia. Among the new delegates were Benjamin Franklin, recently returned from England, and Thomas Jefferson of Virginia. Georgia sent delegates, so for the first time the Congress represented all thirteen colonies. The Continental Congress served as the central government of the colonies for the next six years.

Because fighting had already begun, the Congress's first task was to organize an army and appoint its commander. For the first stage of the war, the colonies had defended themselves with their own militias. What was needed now was a long-term fighting force enlisted to serve not one colony but the whole continent—thus the Continental Army was formed. The Congress appointed George Washington of Virginia as the army's commander in chief.

This document (opposite page, top) is George Washington's commission from the Continental Congress. The document names him "Commander in Chief of the United Colonies and all the forces raised or to be raised by them, and of all others who shall voluntarily offer their services and join the said army."

This Philadelphia building (opposite page, bottom) became the regular meeting place for the Continental Congress for the next six years. It became known as Independence Hall after the Declaration of Independence was signed there in July 1776. This engraving is based on a drawing by Charles Willson Peale.

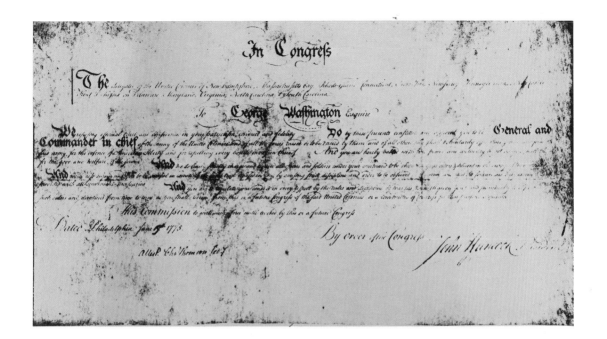

George Washington (1732-99) had gained his reputation as a commander during the French and Indian War. In this nineteenth century engraving (above), he is shown reviewing his troops shortly after taking charge of the Continental Army.

These figures of a revolutionary soldier drilling (this page, above) come from a recruiting poster. To compensate for the hardships of army life, volunteers often received cash bonuses and other rewards. The instruction sheet (opposite page) gives guidelines for officers in charge of new recruits. Instructions include enforcing discipline, keeping costs down, and making sure the new soldiers are in good health.

INSTRUCTIONS for the inlisting of MEN.

FIRST. You are not to inlist any man who is not able-bodied, healthy, and a good marcher; but as men of a good appearance may have ruptures, and venerial complaints, which render them incapable of Soldier's duty; you must give attention, that you be not imposed upon, and take the Opinion of a Surgeon, where there is room for suspicion.

II. You will have great regard to moral character, sobriety in particular,—let our manners distinguish us from our enemies, as much as the cause we are engaged in.

III. Those who engage in defence of their Country's Liberty, shall be inlisted till the last day of December, of the present year, unless sooner discharged by the Continental Congress.

IV. You shall appoint such men Sergeants and Corporals, as recommend themselves by their ability, activity, and diligence.

V. You will use all diligence in completing your company, and report to the President of the Provincial Congress, to the end that you may receive orders to join your regiment.

VI. During the time you are filling up your company, you will engage at the cheapest rate, for the provisions of such men as are already inlisted, if there be no public magazine of provisions, from whence you may be supplied. *not exceeding Eight Shill. p. Week*

VII. You will loose no time in disciplining your men, so far as your situation will admit.

VIII. You will take notice, that proper persons will be appointed to inspect your men, and reject such as do not answer to your instructions.

IX. You will furnish the Subalterns appointed to your company, with a copy of those instructions, who are hereby ordered to put themselves under your command.

X. You will observe, that the troops raised by this Colony will be placed precisely upon the same footing as to pay, clothing, &c. with other the Continental Troops now raised, or hereafter to be raised for the general defence.

XI. No Apprentice or Servant without their Master Consent to be enlisted ———

IN PROVINCIAL CONGRESS at New-York, June 20th 1775.

To *Samuel Broome*   Gentleman, GREETING.

KNOW Ye, That the grand Continental Congress, of the associated Colonies, have Resolved and Ordered, that a certain Number of Troops should be embodied in this Colony, to give Protection to the Inhabitants, and to be employed as Part of the American, Continental Army. WE THEREFORE, reposing special Confidence in your Prudence, Courage, and Affection to the Liberties of this Country, DO request and authorize you, to inlist and raise a Company of seventy-two able bodied sober Men, of good Reputations, (including three Serjeants, three Corporals, one Drummer, and one Fifer,) to serve as Part of the said Troops; and that from Time to Time, you report your Progress in the Premises, to this Congress, for which this shall be your Warrant. And we hereby give you Assurance, that you will be appointed a *Captain* in the said Troops, when raised and embodied, if the Number of Men inlisted by you, (and *Benj. Ledger & Benj. Seipas* — intended to be the other Officers of one Company,) and received into the said Troops, by such proper Officer or Muster-Master, as shall be appointed for that Purpose, shall amount to the Number above-mentioned.

P. V. B. Livingston President

A LAST EFFORT FOR PEACE

Even after war broke out in the spring of 1775, many delegates to the Continental Congress still hoped that the conflict with Britain could still be settled peacefully. On July 5, 1775, the Congress drafted the Olive Branch Petition—a final plea to Britain for a peaceful reconciliation. While the petition respectfully identified the colonies as subjects to the "mother colony," it also asked the British government to answer colonial grievances. When King George III received the petition, he refused to read it. The next day, more radical delegates, led by Thomas Jefferson, submitted a document of a different nature called "A Declaration of the Causes and Necessity of Taking Up Arms." In it, the authors expressed their willingness to fight for their freedom.

John Dickinson (1732-1808; above) was the author of the Olive Branch Petition. Throughout his career he was an influential statesmen and a Patriot. During 1767 and 1768, he wrote a series of articles called Letters from a Farmer in Pennsylvania, *which criticized Britain's policies toward the colonies. Dickinson did not support independence, however, and at the beginning of the war still favored a peaceful settlement with Britain.*

This engraving of George Washington (opposite page) was published in London in 1775. While Congress debated how to appeal for peace with Britain, Washington was busy organizing and training the Continental Army in Massachusetts.

BATTLE SCENES: OCTOBER 1775 TO JUNE 1776

In the fall of 1775, American forces invaded Canada, hoping to divert British troops from New England. The first expedition, led by General Richard Montgomery, captured Montreal in November. In December Montgomery joined another Continental force, led by Benedict Arnold, and attacked Quebec. Outnumbered and exhausted by the difficult journey through the wilderness, the Americans did not succeed in taking the city. Montgomery died in the fighting. The British took many prisoners and forced the remaining Americans to retreat to New England in the spring.

In October 1775, a British naval force attacked Falmouth, Maine, setting the town on fire. Three months later, British warships destroyed the town of Norfolk, Virginia. These raids turned more and more colonists against the English king.

The Americans did achieve several important victories against the British that winter and spring. On March 17, after General Henry Knox arrived in Boston with the captured British cannons, the British army decided to leave the area. Then, on June 28, the Patriots fought off a British naval attack against Charleston, South Carolina.

Sir Guy Carleton (1724-1808; above) was the governor of Quebec and the commander of the British forces in Canada from 1767 to 1783. Under Carleton's leadership, the British withstood the long winter siege of Quebec and succeeded in driving off the American force in late spring of 1776.

The Americans attacked Quebec City on December 31, 1775, shown in this print (opposite page, bottom). The assault, made during a blinding snowstorm, was a failure for the Patriot army.

Benedict Arnold (1741-1801; right) was considered one of the best American officers in the first years of the war. He was wounded in the assault on Quebec City, but he managed to besiege the city until the British drove him out in the spring. Although he went on to achieve important victories, Arnold did not receive the promotions he expected, and in 1780 he betrayed the Americans by going over to the side of the British.

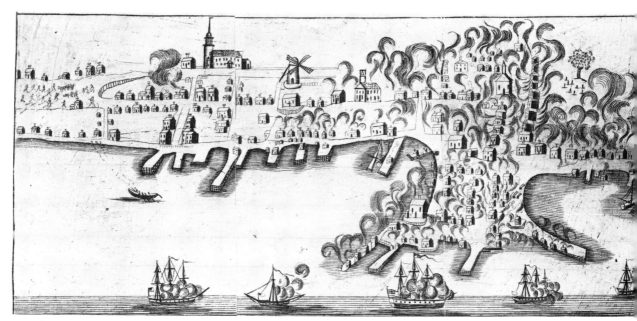

In the winter of 1776, General Henry Knox arrived in Boston with the artillery seized at Fort Ticonderoga. Realizing that they could not withstand such powerful weapons in the hands of the Patriots, the British decided to evacuate their troops from the city. This nineteenth-century illustration (above) shows General Washington watching as the British fleet departs on March 26, 1776. They sailed from Boston to Halifax, Nova Scotia.

On October 16, 1775, the British naval commander Henry Mowat brought several ships into the harbor of Falmouth (later called Portland), Maine. He ordered the citizens to evacuate the town. Two days later Mowat commanded his fleet to open fire, as shown in this engraving (opposite page, top). More than half of Falmouth's two hundred houses were destroyed in the fire.

Both the Americans and British used artillery in the Revolutionary War. In this illustration from a book called A Treatise of Artillery (opposite page, bottom), a soldier loads an explosive shell into a mortar, while another man fires a cannon at the enemy.

Sir Henry Clinton (c.1738-95; left) was a British general who fought in the Battle of Bunker Hill. He was promoted to second-in-command of British forces, and in June 1776, led an unsuccessful attack on Charleston, South Carolina. In 1778 he replaced Sir William Howe as commander in chief of British forces, until 1782.

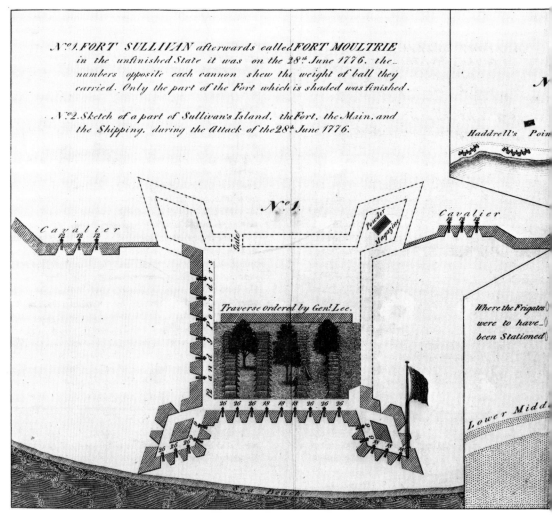

Nº 1. FORT SULLIVAN afterwards called FORT MOULTRIE in the unfinished State it was on the 28ᵗʰ June 1776. the numbers opposite each cannon shew the weight of ball they carried. Only the part of the Fort which is shaded was finished.

Nº 2. Sketch of a part of Sullivan's Island, the Fort, the Main, and the Shipping, during the Attack of the 28ᵗʰ June 1776.

After failing to capture Charleston, British commanders Peter Parker and Henry Clinton faced great embarrassment at home. This British cartoon (right) depicts Fort Sullivan as a hairstyle on top of a lady's head. It is entitled "Miss Carolina Sullivan, one of the most obstinate daughters of America, 1776."

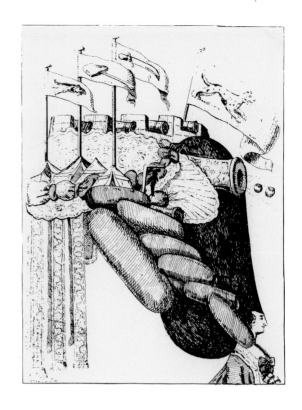

A combined British land and naval force attacked Charleston, South Carolina, on June 28, 1776. American colonel William Moultrie was waiting for them in a log fort on Sullivan's Island, in the city's harbor. The British fleet bombarded Fort Sullivan for twelve hours but failed to drive the Americans out. Moultrie and his troops withstood the attack. This diagram (left) shows an overview of the attack and a plan of the fort.

The Declaration of Independence created a great stir of patriotism among the colonists. This engraving by Andre Basset shows the citizens New York pulling down a statue of King George III after hearing a public reading of the Declaration on July 9, 1776. The statue, made of lead, was then melted down and used for bullets.

The Declaration of Independence defined the purpose of the war. Listing reasons why the colonies should be free, the Declaration made a case for revolution. The war became a major turning point in history.

Meanwhile, the American forces found themselves at a disadvantage—all the economic and military strength was on the side of the British. Among the worst defeats the Continental Army suffered in the war were the Battle of Long Island (August 1776) and the capture of Fort Washington in November. The Patriots, however, won several battles against the Redcoats in New Jersey before retiring for the rest of the winter. These engagements helped boost morale among American soldiers.

It was the American victory at Saratoga in October 1777 that helped change the course of the war. The British generals sought to divide the colonies along the Hudson River. This plan might have succeeded if the leaders, one marching from the north and the other from the south, had reached their meeting point in time. On his own, British general John Burgoyne was unable to penetrate American defenses near Saratoga and surrendered his army after suffering heavy losses. This triumph, America's greatest so far in the war, prevented the British from cutting off New England and encouraged France to aid the colonists.

A TIMELINE OF MAJOR EVENTS

PART II *July 1776-January 1778 Declaring Liberty; Struggling to Survive*

WORLD HISTORY

August 19, 1776 Louis XVI restores forced labor, which had been previously abolished.

September 14 The French make a treaty with the Kilwa sultanate to supply slaves for their sugar plantations in Ile de France and on the Reunion Islands, off the coast of Madagascar in the Indian Ocean.

1776 British author

Louis XVI

Richard Price publishes *Observations on Civil Liberty and War with America,* which angers the upper classes.

1776 Sir William Chambers builds Somerset House in London, to house British archives.

1776 The Tukulor chiefs of Senegal seize power. They are led by Suleiman Bal, who replaces the region's traditional religion with Islam.

1776 Scientist Albrecht von Haller publishes a significant bibliography of 52,000 botanical works.

1776 The first stopwatch is made by Jean-Moyse Pouzait in Geneva, Switzerland.

1776 Famine strikes Bengal, India; one-third of the population dies.

1776 The Marquis of Abban experiments with a steam-powered boat on the Saone River in France.

COLONIAL HISTORY

THE REVOLUTIONARY WAR

July 4 Congress formally adopts the Declaration of Independence. Copies are distributed through- out the colonies to pub- licize the event.

July 8 John Nixon gives the first public reading of the Declaration of Independence in Philadelphia.

July 12 John Dickinson presents his plan for confederation to Congress.

July 20-21 A force of Cherokee Indians attacks a settlement in North Carolina.

August 1 After the British defeat at Charleston, General Clinton's forces join Howe in New York City.

August 2 The Declaration of Independence is signed by the remaining members of the Contin- ental Congress.

August 12 Congress grants free land to British deserters who join the Patriot cause.

August 27-29 In the Battle of Long Island, General Howe's forces defeat Washington's army. Washington withdraws his forces from Brooklyn Heights to Manhattan.

September 6 The world's first submarine attack, by Continental soldier David Bushnell's *Turtle,* fails to sink Admiral Richard Howe's flagship.

September 9 Congress resolves that the words "United States" are to replace "United Colonies."

September 11 British General Howe holds a peace conference with John Adams, Benjamin Franklin, and Edmund Rutledge, which ends in a stalemate.

September 12 Washing- ton evacuates New York City.

September 16 The Continental Army repulses a British attack at Harlem Heights.

September 21 A fire sweeps through New York City, destroying most of its buildings.

September 22 Patriot Nathan Hale is hanged for spying on the British in New York.

September 26 Congress appoints Silas Deane, Benjamin Franklin, and Thomas Jefferson to

Nathan Hale

secure aid from France. Franklin and Deane travel to France, and Arthur Lee later replaces Jefferson.

October 3 Congress issues bills of credit to help finance the war and authorizes Franklin and Deane to borrow money from France.

First public reading of the Declaration of Independence

Charles III

1776 Edward Gibbon publishes the first volume of *The Decline and Fall of the Roman Empire*, scandalizing many readers with his opinion that Christianity was the chief cause of Rome's decline.

1776 Guatemala Nueva (New Guatemala) is founded in Central America.

1776 In Spain, King Charles III appoints the reformist José Moñino, Count of Floridablanca, as his prime minister.

1776 In Vienna, composer

Edward Gibbon

Mozart

Wolfgang Amadeus Mozart composes *Serenade in D* for the marriage of Elizabeth Haffner.

New York City burning

October 11 Benedict Arnold's fleet on Lake Champlain is defeated by a superior British fleet led by General Guy Carleton.

October 13 The British occupy Crown Point, New York.

October 23 Washington leads the main part of his army out of New York City (leaving some men at Fort Washington on northern Manhattan Island) and marches to White Plains.

October 28 British and Patriot forces clash in the Battle of White Plains. Washington's army retreats.

November 16 British and Hessian troops under General Howe capture Fort Washington.

November 19 British forces under General Cornwallis force troops under Nathaniel Greene to evacuate Fort Lee, New Jersey.

December 12 Fearing a British attack on Philadelphia, Congress leaves for Baltimore, where it meets for the next three months.

December 13 American General Charles Lee is captured by a British patrol at Basking Ridge, New Jersey. General John Sullivan assumes control of Lee's forces.

December 19 Thomas Paine publishes *The Crisis*, with its famous first sentence, "These are the times that try men's souls."

December 25-26 In a daring surprise operation, Washington crosses the Delaware River and attacks Hessian troops at Trenton, New Jersey.

December 31 George Rogers Clark petitions Virginia to annex the Kentucky settlement, ruining Daniel Boone's

General Cornwallis and his army

plan to organize Kentucky as a separate state.

January 3, 1777

July 23, 1777

WORLD HISTORY

January, 1777 The first French daily newspaper, the *Journal de Paris,* is published.

February 24 King Joseph of Portugal dies; his daughter, Maria Braganza, takes the throne.

February The Queen Mother of Portugal dismisses the Marquis of Pombal, who expelled the Jesuits from Brazil in 1759, thus reducing the power of the Roman Catholic church in that country.

March Oldenburg is made a dukedom under Frederick Augustus of Holstein-Gottorp.

June 29 Jacques Necker, a French financier, is made Director General of Finance in France. He brings order to the department and devises a more just taxation system.

December 30 Maximilian III of Bavaria dies. Charles Theodore, the Elector of the Palatinate, succeeds him.

1777 French chemist Antoine de Lavoisier perfects his theory of combustion, proving that air consists of oxygen and nitrogen.

1777 Austrian composer Joseph Haydn composes his C-major symphony.

1777 The Perpetual

Alliance between Spain and Portugal settles disputes about their South American colonies.

Antoine de Lavoisier

COLONIAL HISTORY   THE REVOLUTIONARY WAR

The Battle of Princeton

January 3 Washington achieves a second important victory by driving the British out of Princeton, New Jersey.

January 6 The Continental Army goes into winter quarters at Morristown, New Jersey.

March 12 Because Washington has cleared most of New Jersey of British troops, Congress returns to Philadelphia.

April 26 British troops destroy an American

storage depot at Danbury, Connecticut.

April 27 Benedict Arnold

Benedict Arnold

defeats a British force at Ridgefield, Connecticut.

May 20 In the Treaty of DeWitts Corner, the Cherokee Indians give up all of their territory in South Carolina.

June 14 Congress appoints John Paul Jones captain of the warship *Ranger*.
•Congress authorizes a "United States" flag, which has thirteen stars and thirteen alternating white and red stripes.

June 17 British General John Burgoyne begins an invasion of the colonies from Canada, traveling down Lake Champlain and the Hudson River Valley to join General William Howe's troops marching up from New York City.

June 30 British forces under General Howe leave eastern New Jersey for New York.

July 6 General Burgoyne captures Fort

Ticonderoga from American General Arthur St. Clair.

July The Vermont Constitution abolishes slavery.

July 20 The Cherokee Indians give up territory in western North Carolina in the Treaty of Long Island, North Carolina.

July 23 British General Howe sets sail from New York with 15,000 men for Chesapeake Bay to begin a campaign aimed at capturing Philadelphia.

The Marquis de Lafayette

1777 In Britain, John Howard publishes *The State of the Prisons in England and Wales,* calling for reform of the penal system.

1777 Spain completes its occupation of what is today the nation of Uruguay.

1777 Captain James Cook discovers the Sandwich Islands, later known as Hawaii.

1777 Christianity is

Captain James Cook

introduced in Korea.

1777 Portugal strengthens Brazil by giving native Brazilians important government positions and incorporating the state of Maranhao with Brazil.

1777 The University of Palermo, an important center for arts and architecture, is founded in Sicily, in southern Italy.

January 1778 The rulers

of Austria and the Palatinate meet about the partition of Bavaria.

1778 Chile becomes a separate province in the Spanish Empire; it had previously been under Spanish jurisdiction as part of Peru.

1778 France and America negotiate and sign two treaties. Congress ratifies the treaties on May 4.

July 27 A French nobleman, the Marquis de Lafayette, arrives in Philadelphia to volunteer for the American cause. Congress makes him a major general in the Continental Army.
•Settler Jane McCrea is murdered by Burgoyne's Indian allies. The incident prompts many colonists to enlist in the Patriot militia.

General William Howe

August 25 General William Howe lands at the head of Chesapeake

Bay, planning to march on to Philadelphia.

September 9-11 In the Battle of Brandywine, General Howe's forces drive Washington's army back toward Philadelphia.

September 21 American General Anthony Wayne's forces are ambushed by General Howe at Paoli, Pennsylvania.

September 26 The British capture Philadelphia.

October 4-5 In the Battle of Germantown, Pennsylvania, the British defeat Washington's troops.

October 7 In the Second Battle of Saratoga, at Bemis Heights, American General Horatio Gates defeats the forces of General Burgoyne.

October 17 British General Burgoyne surrenders his entire

Burgoyne surrendering to Gates

force to American General Horatio Gates. News of the victory encourages France to join the war on the American side.

November 2 Captain John Paul Jones sails across the Atlantic to raid English ports.

November 15 The Continental Congress approves the Articles of Confederation.

November 17 The Articles of Confederation are sent to the states for ratification. Unanimous ratification is required, but Maryland refuses due to a demand for control over lands west of the Ohio River.

November 1777 San Jose, California, is founded.

December 17 The Continental Army goes into winter quarters at Valley Forge, Pennsylvania.
•France officially recognizes the independence of the American colonies.

December 23 The Conway Cabal, a plot to replace George Washington with Horatio Gates, is revealed. The plot fails and Washington remains head of the Continental Army.

December David Bushnell, inventor of the one–man submarine, lays a minefield to harass British ships around Philadelphia.

February 23, 1778 Prussian officer Baron von Steuben arrives at Valley Forge; he brings discipline and European tactics to the Continental Army.

THE DECLARATION OF INDEPENDENCE

The Olive Branch Petition, the last-ditch effort for peace by the Continental Congress, was flatly rejected by King George III. Many Americans saw no alternative but to break permanently from Britain, and a growing majority of delegates in the Continental Congress favored separation. On June 7, 1776, Richard Henry Lee of Virginia offered a resolution stating that the colonies were "free and independent states."

The members of Congress appointed a committee of Thomas Jefferson, Benjamin Franklin, John Adams, Roger Sherman, and Robert R. Livingston to draft a declaration based on Lee's resolution. The delegates read the statement and met to argue its points for three days beginning July 1. After much heated discussion, they adopted the Declaration of Independence on July 4, 1776. All in all, fifty-six delegates from the thirteen colonies added their signatures to the document. As he signed, Benjamin Franklin remarked, "We must all hang together, or assuredly we shall all hang separately."

There were two main parts to this historic document. The first, the Preamble, stated that "all men are created equal" and possess certain God-given rights such as "Life, Liberty and the pursuit of Happiness." The second part listed British injustices against America. Defending this right presented a different challenge, one the new government and the Continental Army would have to face in the coming months.

As the president of the Continental Congress, John Hancock (1737-93; above) was the first delegate to sign the Declaration. He wrote his name especially large and said, "There, I guess King George will be able to read that!"

Richard Henry Lee (1732-94; right) came from a well-to-do-family in Virginia. In 1758, he was elected to the Virginia House of Burgesses and began his political career defending the rights of the colonies. Lee supported a complete break from Britain in 1776, and it was his resolution that led to the Declaration of Independence.

This engraving (below), after a painting by John Trumbull, shows the five-member committee presenting their document to the Congress. On July 2, the delegates voted to approve the first clause, demanding independence from Britain. Over the next two days, they debated the remaining points, finally signing the Declaration on July 4.

Thomas Jefferson (1743-1826; above) was chosen to write the Declaration of Independence for what John Adams called his "peculiar felicity of expression." Jefferson replied, "I will do as well as I can." A scholar, statesman, philosopher, and architect, Jefferson went on to become the third president of the United States.

Jefferson's first draft of the Declaration (right) contained an attack on slavery, though Jefferson was himself a slaveowner. The delegates from the South opposed banning slavery and deleted this part of the document. Jefferson's harsh language against King George III was also softened in the final draft.

As a formal announcement of separation from the British Crown, the Declaration of Independence (opposite page) marked the birth of a new nation—the United States of America. Jefferson later wrote that he meant the Declaration to be "an expression of the American mind." Using those ideas as the basis for a new society and government marked an important turning point in the Revolutionary War.

In CONGRESS, July 4, 1776.

A DECLARATION

By the REPRESENTATIVES of the

UNITED STATES OF AMERICA,

In GENERAL CONGRESS ASSEMBLED.

WHEN in the Course of human Events, It becomes neceffary for one People to diffolve the Political Bands which have connected them with another, and to affume among the Powers of the Earth, the feparate and equal Station to which the Laws of Nature and of Nature's God entitle them, a decent Refpect to the Opinions of Mankind requires that they fhould declare the caufes which impel them to the Separation.

We hold thefe Truths to be felf-evident, that all Men are created equal, that they are endowed by their Creator with certain unalienable Rights, that among thefe are Life, Liberty, and the Purfuit of Happinefs—That to fecure thefe Rights, Governments are inftituted among Men, deriving their juft Powers from the Confent of the Governed, that whenever any Form of Government becomes deftructive of thefe Ends, it is the Right of the People to alter or to abolifh it, and to inftitute new Government, laying its Foundation on fuch Principles, and organizing its Powers in fuch Form, as to them fhall feem moft likely to effect their Safety and Happinefs. Prudence, indeed, will dictate that Governments long eftablifhed fhould not be changed for light and tranfient Caufes; and accordingly all Experience hath fhewn, that Mankind are more difpofed to fuffer, while Evils are fufferable, than to right themfelves by abolifhing the Forms to which they are accuftomed. But when a long Train of Abufes and Ufurpations, purfuing invariably the fame Object, evinces a Defign to reduce them under abfolute Defpotifm, it is their Right, it is their Duty, to throw off fuch Government, and to provide new Guards for their future Security. Such has been the patient Sufferance of thefe Colonies; and fuch is now the Neceffity which conftrains them to alter their former Syftems of Government. The Hiftory of the prefent King of Great-Britain is a Hiftory of repeated Injuries and Ufurpations, all having in direct Object the Eftablifhment of an abfolute Tyranny over thefe States. To prove this, let Facts be fubmitted to a candid World.

He has refufed his Affent to Laws, the moft wholefome and neceffary for the public Good.

He has forbidden his Governors to pafs Laws of immediate and preffing Importance, unlefs fufpended in their Operation till his Affent fhould be obtained; and when fo fufpended, he has utterly neglected to attend to them.

He has refufed to pafs other Laws for the Accommodation of large Diftricts of People, unlefs thofe People would relinquifh the Right of Reprefentation in the Legiflature, a Right ineftimable to them, and formidable to Tyrants only.

He has called together Legiflative Bodies at Places unufual, uncomfortable, and diftant from the Depofitory of their public Records, for the fole Purpofe of fatiguing them into Compliance with his Meafures.

He has diffolved Reprefentative Houfes repeatedly, for oppofing with manly Firmnefs his Invafions on the Rights of the People.

He has refufed for a long Time, after fuch Diffolutions, to caufe others to be elected; whereby the Legiflative Powers, incapable of Annihilation, have returned to the People at large for their exercife; the State remaining in the mean time expofed to all the Dangers of Invafion from without, and Convulfions within.

H. has endeavoured to prevent the Population of thefe States; for that Purpofe obftructing the Laws for Naturalization of Foreigners; refufing to pafs others to encourage their Migrations hither, and raifing the Conditions of new Appropriations of Lands.

He has obftructed the Adminiftration of Juftice, by refufing his Affent to Laws for eftablifhing Judiciary Powers.

He has made Judges dependent on his Will alone, for the Tenure of their Offices, and the Amount and Payment of their Salaries.

He has erected a Multitude of new Offices, and fent hither Swarms of Officers to harrafs our People, and eat out their Subftance.

He has kept among us, in Times of Peace, Standing Armies, without the confent of our Legiflatures.

He has affected to render the Military independent of and fuperior to the Civil Power.

He has combined with others to fubject us to a Jurifdiction foreign to our Conftitution, and unacknowledged by our Laws; giving his Affent to their Acts of pretended Legiflation:

For quartering large Bodies of Armed Troops among us:

For protecting them, by a mock Trial, from Punifhment for any Murders which they fhould commit on the Inhabitants of thefe States:

For cutting off our Trade with all Parts of the World:

For impofing Taxes on us without our Confent:

For depriving us, in many Cafes, of the Benefits of Trial by Jury:

For transporting us beyond Seas to be tried for pretended Offences:

For abolifhing the free Syftem of Englifh Laws in a neighbouring Province, eftablifhing therein an arbitrary Government, and enlarging its Boundaries, fo as to render it at once an Example and fit Inftrument for introducing the fame abfolute Rule into thefe Colonies:

For taking away our Charters, abolifhing our moft valuable Laws, and altering fundamentally the Forms of our Governments:

For fufpending our own Legiflatures, and declaring themfelves invefted with Power to legiflate for us in all Cafes whatfoever.

He has abdicated Government here, by declaring us out of his Protection and waging War againft us.

He has plundered our Seas, ravaged our Coafts, burnt our Towns, and deftroyed the Lives of our People.

He is, at this Time, transporting large Armies of foreign Mercenaries to compleat the Works of Death, Defolation, and Tyranny, already begun with circumftances of Cruelty and Perfidy, fcarcely paralleled in the moft barbarous Ages, and totally unworthy the Head of a civilized Nation.

He has conftrained our fellow Citizens taken Captive on the high Seas to bear Arms againft their Country, to become the Executioners of their Friends and Brethren, or to fall themfelves by their Hands.

He has excited domeftic Infurrections amongft us, and has endeavoured to bring on the Inhabitants of our Frontiers, the mercilefs Indian Savages, whofe known Rule of Warfare, is an undiftinguifhed Deftruction, of all Ages, Sexes and Conditions.

In every ftage of thefe Oppreffions we have Petitioned for Redrefs in the moft humble Terms: Our repeated Petitions have been answered only by repeated Injury. A Prince, whofe Character is thus marked by every act which may define a Tyrant, is unfit to be the Ruler of a free People.

Nor have we been wanting in Attentions to our Britifh Brethren. We have warned them from Time to Time of Attempts by their Legiflature to extend an unwarrantable Jurifdiction over us. We have reminded them of the Circumftances of our Emigration and Settlement here. We have appealed to their native Juftice and Magnanimity, and we have conjured them by the Ties of our common Kindred to difavow thefe Ufurpations, which, would inevitably interrupt our Connections and Correfpondence. They too have been deaf to the Voice of Juftice and of Confanguinity. We muft, therefore, acquiefce in the Neceffity, which denounces our Separation, and hold them, as we hold the reft of Mankind, Enemies in War, in Peace, Friends.

We, therefore, the Reprefentatives of the UNITED STATES OF AMERICA, in GENERAL CONGRESS, Affembled, appealing to the Supreme Judge of the World for the Rectitude of our Intentions, do, in the Name, and by Authority of the good People of thefe Colonies, folemnly Publifh and Declare, That thefe United Colonies are, and of Right ought to be, FREE AND INDEPENDENT STATES; that they are abfolved from all Allegiance to the Britifh Crown, and that all political Connection between them and the State of Great-Britain, is and ought to be totally diffolved; and that as FREE AND INDEPENDENT STATES, they have full Power to levy War, conclude Peace, contract Alliances, eftablifh Commerce, and to do all other Acts and Things which INDEPENDENT STATES may of right do. And for the fupport of this Declaration, with a firm Reliance on the Protection of divine Providence, we mutually pledge to each other our Lives, our Fortunes, and our facred Honor.

Signed by ORDER and in BEHALF of the CONGRESS,

JOHN HANCOCK, PRESIDENT.

ATTEST.
CHARLES THOMSON, SECRETARY.

PHILADELPHIA: PRINTED BY JOHN DUNLAP.

117

The first public reading of the Declaration of Independence took place in Philadelphia, outside Independence Hall, on July 8, 1776. John Adams wrote that the people were excited, and "the bells rang all day and almost all night." This engraving (below) appeared in an 1876 edition of Harper's Weekly *honoring America's centennial.*

Once the new nation declared its independence, it needed to establish its own government. Benjamin Franklin addressed this problem as early as July 1775, a year before the colonies proclaimed their freedom from Britain. Franklin proposed that the colonies unite and form a confederation, which would then work as a central government for the United States. Jefferson wrote down Franklin's ideas and added his own notes in this draft (left).

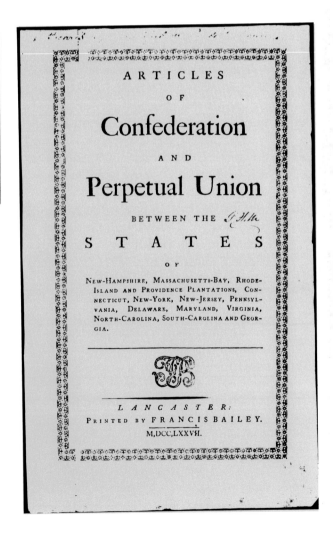

Congress approved the Articles of Confederation in November 1777, and the United States ratified them in March 1781. The Articles, though often criticized as weak, helped keep the new nation together until 1789, when a stronger system of government was established by the Constitution of the United States. Shown here (right) is the first page of the Articles.

THE PLIGHT OF THE LOYALISTS

Even after July 1776, the American colonies remained divided on the issue of independence. Historians do not know the exact percentage of the population either for or against rebellion, but they generally agree that roughly one third of the colonists were Patriots, one third Loyalists, and one third neutral. The Patriots generally supported the Revolutionary War, but not all of them believed in the cause for national independence. They fought when war came into their own areas, but were often hesitant to join the army's ranks to defend other regions.

The Loyalists, who were also called Tories, wanted to remain loyal to the British Crown. Some were simply uneasy about change, while others were unwilling to take such a bold and dangerous step as openly declaring war on England. Many Loyalists thought the wisest action was to tolerate the British government and King George III. Although Loyalists came from different regions and social classes, many of them were prominent citizens.

Patriotic groups harrassed the Loyalists, considering them a threat to the Revolutionary cause. Tories suffered ridicule, beating, and sometimes even death, at the hands of their Patriot counterparts, while Patriot mobs and local governments siezed their property. More than sixty thousand Loyalists left America for England, while others fled to Canada or set sail for British colonies in the West Indies.

"Neighbor was against neighbor, father against son and son against father," one *Connecticut Loyalist said. "He that would not thrust his own blade through his brother's heart was called an infamous villain." The differences that divided Loyalist from Patriot were sometimes unclear, yet their clashes were often bitter and bloody. This illustration (above) appeared in* M'Fingal, *a popular eighteenth-century satire by John Trumbull. In it an English sympathizer is "strung up" and ridiculed by his Patriot neighbors.*

Although many in England were sympathetic to the Loyalists' difficult situation in America, the Loyalists received little support, guidance, or direction from the British government before 1778. This British cartoon (above) criticizes the government's neglect by showing an "ungrateful Briton" leaving his "loyal friends" to the ravages of the Americans.

This illustration (right), also from M'Fingal, entitled "Tory Pandemonium," shows a group of Loyalists discussing the situation in the colonies. The prospect of breaking from England caused worry and fear among the Loyalists. Many of them decided to serve in the regular British army while others fought in their own Loyalist units, set up by Crown supporters throughout the colonies.

THE BATTLE OF LONG ISLAND AND CAPTURE OF FORT WASHINGTON

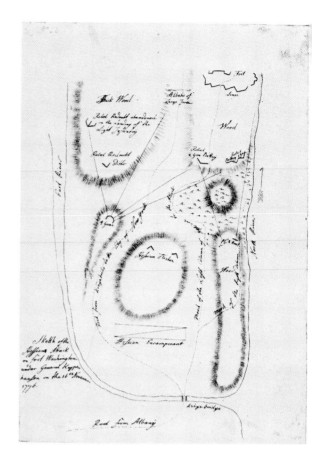

The Battle of Long Island marked the beginning of the struggle between British and American forces for New York City. On July 2, 1776, the British, under General William Howe, landed ten thousand men on Staten Island. By August, the force had grown to 32,000 men. Howe's brother, Admiral Richard Howe, commanded a large fleet of warships and transports. Outnumbered on both land and sea, General George Washington sent nineteen thousand men to defend the western end of Long Island.

In the early morning of August 27, 1776, the British stormed American positions. American resistance collapsed. Washington lost over a thousand men, Howe only four hundred. Washington saved his men from total defeat by crossing the East River into Manhattan.

Washington retreated north into Westchester County, leaving about three thousand men at Fort Washington in northern Manhattan. On October 28, at the Battle of White Plains, British troops again defeated the Americans. Instead of pursuing Washington into New Jersey, Howe turned to Manhattan and attacked Fort Washington. The British captured the fort and took control of Manhattan Island.

This drawing (above) shows the route of the Hessian attack against Fort Washington on the morning of November 16, 1776. The Hessians were soldiers from Germany used by King George III to complete his royal army. The soldiers from Hesse were generally well-trained and disciplined. After a savage battle, the German soldiers captured the fort for the British.

General William Howe (1729-1814), pictured here in an engraving by Johann Probst (above), was commander in chief of British forces in America from October 1775 to May 1778. In the Battle of Long Island, he missed the chance to end the war in one blow by refusing to destroy the last remnants of Washington's army.

The struggle for strategic New York City was costly for both sides. The broadside (a published public announcement) at right lists the British dead and wounded from the battles of White Plains and Fort Washington. The list later appeared in an eighteenth-century British book, The History of the War in America Between Great Britain and Her Colonies, from its Commencement to the End of the Year 1778.

A LIST of the Killed, Wounded, and Missing of His Majesty's Forces, under the Command of his Excellency the Honourable General HOWE, in the several Engagements and Skirmishes with the PROVINCIALS, from the taking of Long-Island, August 27th, to the Close of that Campaign, the 8th December, 1776.

THE REDCOATS TAKE NEW YORK CITY

In September 1776, General Howe and his British-Hessian troops took over New York City. Crowds of Loyalists cheered the British victory, then quickly turned on their Patriot neighbors. On the morning of September 21, a fire broke out, wreaking havoc upon citizens and soldiers alike. The blaze raged through the streets, destroying five hundred buildings. The origin of the fire remains a mystery, but the British and Tories believed it to be a rebel plot. General Washington had actually considered an idea suggested by Nathaniel Greene to burn the city rather than turn it over to the British. He rejected the plan but said later, "Providence, or some good honest fellow, has done more for us than we were disposed to do for ourselves." Suspects were rounded up and some were hanged without a trial, while others were thrown back into the blaze to their deaths.

Charred and gutted by fire, New York City was now of little value to General Howe. One Loyalist wrote that New York was "a most dirty, desolate and wretched place." Life was particularly difficult for the Patriots imprisoned there. The conditions inspired much resentment among Patriots outside the city and convinced many Loyalists to change sides. The British occupied the city for seven years. New York became known as the Tory capital of America for the remainder of the Revolutionary War.

The etching below shows the parade of the British army through New York City in mid-September 1776. The arrival of the victorious British troops sparked a wave of fear among the defeated Patriots. Tories seized and imprisoned anyone remotely suspected of supporting the Patriot cause. From the battles of Long Island and Fort Washington, the British took more than 4,400 prisoners and kept them in makeshift jails, churches, warehouses, and rotting ships around the city.

AN AUDACIOUS VICTORY, A BITTER DEFEAT

Preferring to spend the winter of 1776-1777 in New York City, General Howe gave over the pursuit of the American army to Lord Charles Cornwallis. Unlike Howe, Cornwallis acted quickly, chasing the remainder of Washington's troops into New Jersey. Once again, Washington escaped defeat, this time by crossing the Delaware River into Pennsylvania. As the British approached Philadelphia, the Continental Congress fled to Baltimore.

Desperate for a victory, General Washington decided to attempt a surprise attack. On Christmas night 1776, with about 2,400 troops, Washington crossed back over the Delaware River and marched to Trenton, New Jersey. At dawn the Americans surprised the British and Hessian troops who were recovering from their Christmas celebration. About 920 Hessians were captured, 25 killed and 90 wounded. The triumph boosted morale and secured Washington's reputation as a military leader. On January 3, 1777, Washington led his troops to Princeton, New Jersey, attacked the British and captured the town.

One year later, in a similar surprise attack, the British avenged these losses by defeating an American force under General Anthony Wayne near Paoli, Pennsylvania. In the dead of night, the Redcoats overwhelmed the Americans, killing or wounding about three hundred men and capturing a hundred more.

A German engraving (above) shows Hessian troops captured at the Battle of Trenton. General Washington paraded nine hundred prisoners through the streets of Philadelphia, almost starting a riot among citizens who resented and feared the Hessian soldiers.

The Americans were camped about two miles to the southwest of the town of Paoli, Pennsylvania, as shown at the center of this map (opposite page, bottom). British forces, under Major General Charles Grey, were ordered to unload their muskets so no accidental shots would warn the Americans of their approach. Using bayonets, the British "quietly" slaughtered many of Wayne's men.

A nineteenth-century print (above) shows General Washington's famous crossing of the Delaware River. After landing, the troops endured a grueling nine-mile march to Trenton. Washington's threadbare army left bloody footprints in the snow, but went on to capture the Hessian troops.

General Anthony Wayne (1745-96), pictured at right, commanded the American troops at Paoli. Nicknamed "Mad Anthony" for his daring exploits during battle, General Wayne got revenge for the Paoli massacre by capturing the British fort at Stony Point, New York, in 1779.

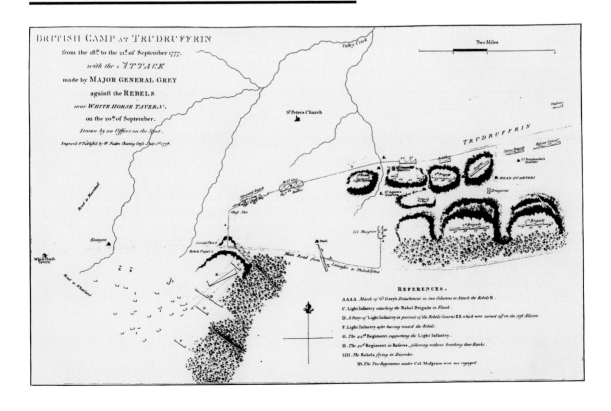

SARATOGA: THE TURNING POINT

By September 1777, British general John Burgoyne had led 7,700 British and Hessian troops from Canada into northern New York. Burgoyne defeated American forces at Fort Ticonderoga on July 6, 1777. He lost about eight hundred men in a battle at Bennington, Vermont. By the time he reached Saratoga, New York, he had 6,500 men left.

While General Burgoyne marched south from Canada, General Howe was supposed to march north from New York City and meet Burgoyne near Albany. This plan was designed to split New England from the middle and southern colonies. Instead, General Howe marched south to Pennsylvania, seeking to attack Washington's troops. Howe captured Philadelphia but failed to crush Washington's army. The series of battles which took place near Saratoga in September and October ended in victory for the Americans. On October 17, 1777, General Burgoyne surrendered his remaining force of about five thousand men to General Horatio Gates.

General Horatio Gates (c.1728-1806), shown in this engraving (above) from An Impartial History of the War in America, *an eighteenth-century history book, was hailed as a hero for defeating John Burgoyne. After the victory, many Americans thought Gates should replace Washington as commander in chief.*

Completely surrounded by Gates's men, Burgoyne realized his only option was to surrender. The etching (below) from Thomas Anburey's Travels through the Interior Parts of America *shows the British encampment after the battles around Saratoga, New York, in 1777.*

At Bemis Heights near Saratoga, in what was called the Second Battle of Freeman's Farm, the British were held off by General Gates, Benedict Arnold, Daniel Morgan, and Benjamin Lincoln. Lincoln (above, left) was named commander of American forces in the South in 1778.

Before leaving for America, General John Burgoyne (1722-92; above, right) bet a friend fifty guineas that he would put down the American rebels within a year's time. With his defeat at Saratoga, Burgoyne lost his bet.

The engraving below shows General Burgoyne offering Gates his sword in a traditional surrender. Gates returned the sword and invited Burgoyne to dinner.

THE LONG WINTER AT VALLEY FORGE

During the eighteenth century, battles were fought according to the seasons. When the weather turned cold, both sides stopped fighting and sought out winter quarters. Washington chose to "winter" his troops at Valley Forge, Pennsylvania, twenty-five miles northwest of Philadelphia. The Continental Army, numbering eleven thousand troops in December 1777, dwindled to four thousand by the time they left camp in June 1778. The soldiers endured many hardships, suffering through blizzards, mud, and epidemics of typhus and other diseases. They lacked proper shelter, food, clothing, and medical supplies. Many soldiers deserted, and fear of a possible mutiny spread among Washington's officers.

In February 1778, Baron Wilhelm von Steuben arrived at Valley Forge. Formerly a Prussian army officer, Steuben drilled the Valley Forge troops daily and improved their discipline. On June 19, 1778, after six long months in camp, the Continental Army left Valley Forge well-trained and much better prepared for the task of fighting the British.

Baron Friedrich Wilhelm von Steuben (1730-94; above) played an important role in training America's inexperienced Continental Army. After meeting with Benjamin Franklin, he traveled from France to help the American side. A soldier since the age of sixteen, Steuben was responsible for molding Washington's army into a veteran fighting force. He wrote Regulations for the Order and Discipline of the Troops of the United States *(1779), a book that was used by the U.S. Army until the War of 1812.*

This nineteenth-century illustration (below) shows General Washington, von Steuben, and some Continental soldiers during the winter at Valley Forge. Lacking proper clothing, the men wrapped themselves in rags to keep warm. The British, meanwhile, were faring better at their more comfortable winter quarters in Philadelphia.

Part III: February 1778-February 1783
Triumphs of Diplomacy and Arms

Benjamin Franklin traveled to France in December 1776 on a mission to win support for the Revolution. It was not until February 1778, several months after hearing news of the American victory at Saratoga, that the French agreed to a treaty of alliance with the United States. This German engraving (left) shows Franklin bidding farewell to King Louis XVI after signing the treaty.

Saratoga was the turning point of the American Revolution. Burgoyne's defeat made the King, Parliament, and the British people realize that defeat at the hands of the Patriot "rabble" was a possibility.

Britain was not the only European nation to take notice of what had happened at Saratoga. As always, the politics of the Old World influenced events in the New World. France, Holland, and Spain—all enemies of Britain to different degrees—had been sending help to the Patriots, hoping to weaken Britain by aiding its enemy. After the American victory at Saratoga, France openly allied itself with the new United States. By the end of the decade, the French were sending a steady supply of soldiers, ships, and money across the Atlantic.

But Britain wasn't ready to give up the fight just yet. As the 1770s ended, British forces won control of much of the southern colonies. However, a spirited guerrilla campaign kept the pressure on the British. Combined with the better-trained, more effective Continental Army that emerged from Valley Forge, these guerilla forces drove the British into an ever-smaller area. Finally, in October 1781, General Cornwallis' army found itself trapped at York-town, Virginia. Cornwallis surrendered, and the British hope of victory disappeared.

Two years later, a peace treaty was signed in Paris. The goal of American independence, after almost a decade of struggle and hardship, had been achieved. The world had witnessed the birth of a new nation—the United States of America.

A TIMELINE OF MAJOR EVENTS

PART III *February 1778–February 1783 Triumphs of Diplomacy and Arms*

WORLD HISTORY

Voltaire

May 30, 1778 French writer and philosopher Voltaire dies at the age of eighty-four.

French warships

June 21 Spain declares war on Britain.

July 2 Jean-Jacques Rousseau, the French-Swiss political philosopher, dies.

July 10 France declares war against Great Britain.

December King Louis XVI attempts financial reform by withdrawing privileges for the nobility in hopes of reducing his country's financial problems; reform proves unpopular with the upper classes.

February 1779 Lafayette returns from America to France to ask the king for more money for the American rebels.

March 31 Russia and Turkey sign a treaty in which both promise to take no military action in the Crimean Peninsula.

April 12 By a secret treaty signed at Aranjuez, Spain is guaranteed a number of advantages if it joins France in supporting the American colonies.

COLONIAL HISTORY

General Henry Clinton

May 8 General Henry Clinton replaces General Howe as overall commander of British forces in the colonies. He plans to evacuate Philadelphia, fearing a blockade by French ships.

May 15 George Rogers Clark begins a campaign to drive British forces and pro-British Indians from the western territories.

June 6 A British peace commission arrives in Philadelphia; Congress rejects their terms for an end to the fighting.

THE REVOLUTIONARY WAR

June 18 British General Henry Clinton leaves Philadelphia and marches his troops to New York City.

June 19 Washington breaks camp at Valley Forge and sends General Charles Lee to attack Clinton's forces.

June 27-28 At the Battle of Monmouth, Washington's men and Clinton's forces fight to a stand-off. Washington is furious at his general, Charles Lee, for ordering a retreat; Lee is later dismissed from the army. Clinton's forces continue on to New York.

July 9 Seven colonies sign the Articles of Confederation. The remaining colonies sign over the next eleven months.
•A British naval force raids and burns Fairfield and then Norwalk, Connecticut.

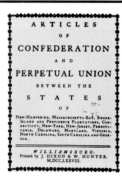

Articles of Confederation

July 20 George Rogers Clark captures the British fort at Vincennes, Indiana.

August 8 Led by General John Sullivan and the French fleet of Count d'Estaing, Patriot forces unsuccessfully try to seize British-held Newport, Rhode Island.

September 14 Congress appoints Benjamin Franklin as American minister (chief diplomat) to France.

December 10 Attorney John Jay of New York is elected president of the Congress.

December 29 The British begin a campaign in the South with the capture of Savannah, Georgia, from American General Robert Howe.

January 10, 1779 John Paul Jones receives a ship from the French, which he refits, and renames the *Bonhomme*

John Paul Jones

Richard, in honor of Benjamin Franklin's *Poor Richard's Almanac.*

January 29 The British capture Augusta, Georgia.

August 10 Louis XVI frees the remaining serfs (members of the class of peasants who were bound to the land by law) on royal lands.

1779 The British capture the island of St. Lucia and force the French fleet led by Admiral d'Estaing to withdraw to Martinique.

1779 Benjamin Robins, an English scientist, contributes in his book, *New Principles of*

Gunnery, to the introduction of carronades, a smaller type of cannon for use on warships.

February 1780 Catherine II of Russia appeals to European countries to support the American Revolution in the League of Armed Neutrality against Britain, which has been attacking those ships not involved in the war.

May 11 Negotiations begin between Spain

and America because France has been pressuring Spain to support the rebels' cause.

June Catherine II and Austrian Emperor Josef II meet to discuss new conquests in the Ottoman Empire.

August 24 France abolishes the use of torture to force criminal suspects to confess.

November 20 England declares war on

Holland, a member of the League of Armed Neutrality.

1780 India's newspaper, the *Bengal Gazette,* edited by James Hickey, begins publication.

1780 The Gordon Riots, violent anti-Catholic demonstrations, take place in London as a result of Parliament lifting restrictions on English Roman Catholics in the Catholic Relief Act.

June 1 British General Henry Clinton captures forts at Stony Point and Verplanck, New York, but fails to reach West Point.

September 3-October 28 American General Benjamin Lincoln withdraws with heavy casualties after an attempt to recapture Savannah, Georgia, fails; Polish-born Continental Army officer Count Casimir Pulaski is killed and French Admiral Count d'Estaing is wounded in the battle.

September 23 John Paul Jones, commanding the *Bonhomme Richard*, captures the British warship *Serapis* in a hard-fought battle.

September 27 Congress appoints John Adams to negotiate peace with Britain. Congress also names John Jay as minister to Spain.

September, 1779 Spanish Governor

John Adams

Bernardo de Galvez of Louisiana captures British forts along the Gulf of Mexico and the Mississippi River.

October 17 Washington leads his men into winter quarters at Morristown, New Jersey, where the soldiers suffer even worse hardships than during the winter at Valley Forge.

November 29 Congress issues more money to finance the war.

May 12, 1780 American General Benjamin

Lincoln surrenders Charleston, South Carolina, to the British in a major defeat for the American cause.

June 13 Congress commissions Horatio Gates as leader of the Continental Army in the Southern colonies.

June 23 In the Battle of Springfield, New Jersey, American forces, led by General Nathanael Greene, defeat the British.

July 11 Led by Count de Rochambeau, 5,000 French soldiers arrive in Newport, Rhode Island.

August 3 Benedict Arnold is appointed commander of West Point; Arnold has been conspiring with the British since 1779 and plans to hand over maps of the fort to the British.

September 8 British forces under Cornwallis begin the invasion of

North Carolina.

September 23 British Major John André is captured with the plans of West Point provided by Benedict Arnold.

September 25 Hearing of André's capture, Benedict Arnold flees from West Point to a British ship. He becomes a Brigadier General in the British Army.

October 7 At King's Mountain, North Carolina, a Loyalist force is defeated by American militia. The loss convinces British General Cornwallis to give up his invasion of North Carolina.

October 14 General Nathanael Greene replaces Horatio Gates as commander of the Patriot forces in the South.

A TIMELINE OF MAJOR EVENTS

PART III *February 1778–February 1783 Triumphs of Diplomacy and Arms*

WORLD HISTORY

February 3, 1781 During the war declared by the British on the Dutch, the British capture the Dutch island of St. Eustatius in the West Indies.

May French finance minister Necker resigns after failing to gain the position of minister of state. His departure shakes the confidence of the French *Bourse* (stock exchange).

•Czarina Catherine II of Russia and Emperor Josef II set up a defensive alliance against the Ottoman (Turkish) Empire.
•Prussia joins the League of Armed Neutrality.

July 1 In the second Mysore War in India, Haidar Ali, the Moslem ruler, is defeated at Porto Nuevo by the British.

1781 The British

Warren Hastings

Governor General of India, Warren Hastings, founds Calcutta Madrassah, a college designed to foster Arabic studies.

1781 In Mozambique, Africa, the Portuguese take the fort of Laurenco Marques back from Austria and resume control of the slave trade from the southern Mozambique coast to Brazil, the French Indian Ocean islands, and Arabia.

COLONIAL HISTORY THE REVOLUTIONARY WAR

February 20, 1781 Congress appoints Robert Morris as superintendent of finance; he takes control on May 14.

March 1 The states formally ratify the Articles of Confederation. Maryland is the last to sign, and the Articles are put into effect for all the states.

March 15 In the Battle of Guilford Courthouse, in North Carolina, the British under General Cornwallis achieve victory, but suffer heavy losses from American forces under General Greene and General Morgan.

March 18 Cornwallis retreats to Wilmington, Delaware, to wait for reinforcements from General Clinton.

April 25 Cornwallis begins the British occupation of Virginia.

May 9 With the British surrender of Pensacola, Spanish forces conquer all of West Florida.

May 26 Congress approves Robert Morris's plan for a Bank of North America, the nation's first bank. Its official opening is December 31.

June 4 British Colonel Banastre Tarleton almost captures Virginia governor Thomas Jefferson at Charlottesville.

June 10 American forces under Marquis de Lafayette in Virginia are joined by General Anthony Wayne's men. Baron von Steuben joins them on June 19. The combined force combats raids by Benedict Arnold and General Cornwallis.

August 1 Cornwallis arrives at Yorktown, Virginia, to set up a base of operations.

August 10 Congress names Robert Livingston Secretary for Foreign Affairs.

August 14 Washington decides to lead his and Rochambeau's men to Philadelphia.

August 30 Count de Grasse's French fleet arrives off the coast of Virginia.

August 31 French troops join Lafayette's American troops to cut off Cornwallis.

September 1 The forces of Rochambeau and Washington reach Philadelphia.

September 5-8 Count de Grasse defeats the British fleet in a naval battle in Chesapeake Bay.

September 6 Benedict Arnold loots and burns New London, Connecticut.

September 8 American forces under General Greene are defeated at Eutaw Springs, South Carolina, but they are still able to push the British back toward Charleston.

September 14-24 Count de Grasse sends ships to transport the forces of Washington and Rochambeau to Virginia.

September 28 The allied army of Americans and French begin the siege of Yorktown.

Surrender at Yorktown

1781 The Suurveld War between Boer ranchers and the Khosian and Xhosa people in South Africa ends in success for the Boers.

1781 The Emperor Josef II publishes "The Edict of Toleration for Protestant and Orthodox Christians."

1781 The construction of the Siberian highway begins in Russia.

1781 German astronomer

William Herschel discovers the planet Uranus, using a reflecting telescope he built himself.

October 22 Louis Joseph, the son of Louis XVI and Marie Antoinette, is born.

1782 The Irish Parliament is made independent of Great Britain.

1782 The Treaty of Salbai ends the Maratha War in India.

1782 Bread riots break out in England.

February 1783 Spain, Sweden, and Denmark recognize the independence of the United States of America.

1783 French inventors, the Montgolfier brothers, build the first hot air balloon which makes a ten-minute ascent.

Marie Antoinette

October 19 General Cornwallis surrenders his entire force, marking the end of British hopes for victory in America.

November 5 The Netherlands extend a large loan to the United States.

December 31 The Bank of North America is officially chartered.

Loyalist Cartoon

January 1, 1782 Thousands of Loyalists begin to leave America, especially from the New England states; many settle in Canada.

January 5 British forces begin to withdraw from the American territory they have occupied during the war.

Peace negotiation

April 12 Peace talks begin between Britain and America. British representatives meet in Paris with Benjamin Franklin.

May 9 Sir Guy Carleton arrives in New York to take over command of British forces left in America from General Henry Clinton.

June 11 British forces evacuate Savannah, Georgia.

August 15 A force of 240 Indians and Canadians unsuccessfully attack Bryan's Station, an American fort in Kentucky. The

Americans, led by Daniel Boone, pursue their attackers and drive them north, back across the Ohio River.

October 8 The Netherlands and the United States sign a treaty of commerce and friendship.

November 30 In Paris, American and British representatives sign a preliminary peace treaty.

December 14 British forces evacuate Charleston, South Carolina.

December 15 France objects to not being consulted by the Americans before signing the preliminary peace treaty with Britain.

January 20, 1783 A preliminary treaty is signed between England and France and between England and Spain; the treaty between England and the United States will not go into effect until the French finalize their settlement with the British.

THE FRENCH ALLIANCE

Britain and France were long-time enemies. The Americans knew this and hoped for military and financial help from France in their struggle against Britain. Shortly after the war began, the French foreign minster, the Comte de Vergennes, convinced King Louis XVI to allow secret aid to the Americans. Vergennes set up a fake "trading company" which began shipping guns, ammunition, and clothing to the Continental Army in 1776. Benjamin Franklin, who was admired and loved by the French, played a major role in obtaining this aid. However, the French government was unwilling to risk war with Britain by giving aid more openly or sending troops to fight. Also, some members of the French government doubted the Americans could win a war against Britain even with French help.

This attitude changed after the American victory at Saratoga in 1777. Also, the French were disturbed by rumors that Britain might soon seek peace with the Americans. This would rob them of the chance to damage their old enemy by helping the Americans. In February 1778, American and French diplomats signed treaties of alliance in Paris. France also recognized the United States as a new nation, becoming the first European nation to do so formally. Spain and Holland, also enemies of Britain, began sending aid to America as well. The news cheered George Washington's Continental Army, which was suffering through a cruel winter at Valley Forge.

Benjamin Franklin (1706-90), pictured at the age of fifty-six in this engraving after a French painting (above), promoted the American cause in France from 1777 to 1785. His charm, wit, and diplomatic skills helped to secure about $60 million in French aid for the Patriot cause.

A British cartoon (opposite page, bottom) shows British peace commissioners asking America (represented by a Native American) for peace in the summer of 1778. The cartoon states the reasons why America should accept Britain's friendly terms. America, with France now on her side, rejects Britain's offer.

Charles Gravier, the Comte de Vergennes (1717-87; right), started a secret company called "Hortalez & Sons" to smuggle money and supplies into America. American independence was a popular cause with French nobles and intellectuals, a fact that Vergennes used to his—and America's—advantage. Among the company's secret agents was Caron de Beaumarchais, one of France's leading playwrights.

Many people in Britain felt it was hypocritical for the Americans to accept French aid. After all, these critics said, the Americans claimed to be fighting for liberty, but the French monarchy was even more tyrannical than Britain's. According to the text accompanying this engraving (above), the alliance made the Americans "dupes to France," and would cause America to end up in "French and Spanish chains."

A contemporary engraving by Noel le Mire shows Marie Joseph Paul Yves Roche Gilbert du Motier, the Marquis de Lafayette (1757-1834; right), a nineteen-year-old French nobleman who volunteered for the Continental Army in 1776. Lafayette proved to be an able and courageous officer and was promoted to major-general the following year. Lafayette became a close friend and trusted adviser to George Washington.

French military aid on both land and sea was of vital importance to the American cause. A contemporary French engraving (below) shows the arrival of a French fleet to assist the American attack on Newport, Rhode Island, in the summer of 1778.

AN AMERICAN NAVAL VICTORY

Captain John Paul Jones was the hero of America's sea war with Britain. The French had given Jones an old merchant ship called the *Duras* which he renamed the *Bonhomme Richard* in honor of Ben Franklin. ("Bonhomme Richard" was the French translation of "Poor Richard," as in the title of Franklin's popular *Poor Richard's Almanac*.) In 1778 Jones captured the HMS *Drake*, the first British warship to surrender to an American vessel. In August and September of 1779, Jones attacked ships in the waters around Britain and Ireland, even raiding coastal towns. But Jones's greatest triumph came in 1779 when he forced the British warship *Serapis* to surrender.

On September 23, 1779, the *Bonhomme Richard* encountered the powerful British warship *Serapis* in the English Channel. The two ships exchanged cannon fire for hours, heavily damaging both vessels. Finally Jones rammed the *Bonhomme Richard* into the *Serapis* and the two crews fought hand-to-hand. In the heat of the battle, British Captain Richard Pearson called on Jones to surrender. Jones replied, "I have not yet begun to fight." After three and a half hours of fierce combat, the *Serapis* surrendered. Jones abandoned the sinking *Bonhomme Richard*, boarded the British ship and sailed her into a French port. The battle was one of America's greatest naval victories, and Jones's reply to the British captain became a rallying cry for the American cause.

John Paul Jones, born in Scotland in 1747, is pictured (above) in this contemporary engraving by Carl Guttenberg from a drawing by C. J. Notte. After the Revolutionary War, the adventurous Jones became an admiral in the Russian Navy. He died in Paris in 1792.

THE LAST EVENTS IN THE NORTH

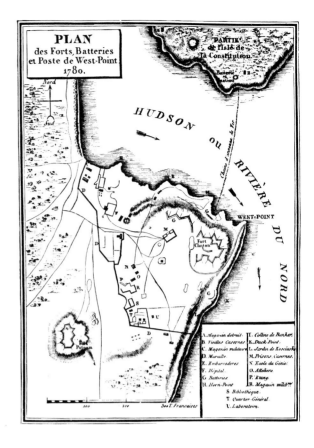

A few weeks before French troops arrived to reinforce Washington's army, British forces left Philadelphia to join forces with Sir Henry Clinton's army in New York City. Washington left Valley Forge in pursuit, and in June 1778, the British and Continental armies met at Monmouth Court House, New Jersey. American General Charles Lee engaged the British in combat but suddenly ordered a retreat. Washington, furious, rode in to take command of the fighting and the Americans escaped a serious defeat.

The Continental forces had survived Valley Forge, and thanks to Baron von Steuben's training, they had faced the British army on the battlefield as equals. Monmouth Court House was the last major battle in the northern colonies, but not the last important event to take place in the region.

In the summer of 1780, General Benedict Arnold became commander of West Point, a key post in America's defense of the Hudson River. Arnold had served the American cause well, but he had grown bitter when he didn't receive the promotions he felt he deserved. While in command of West Point, Arnold secretly met with a British officer, Major John André. Hoping for high rank in the British army, Arnold handed over plans of the American fort to Major André. However, American troops captured André and found the plans. Arnold fled to a British ship, and André was hanged.

A contemporary map (above) shows the strategic American fortifications at West Point. The map also shows a huge iron chain stretching across the Hudson. George Washington had the chain constructed to keep British ships from moving up the river.

Benedict Arnold (1741-1801) received the rank of brigadier general in the British Army. However, he received only a fraction of the money he expected in return for his treason. Shortly after going over to the British, Arnold issued this broadside (opposite page) in an attempt to lure American soldiers to the side of the British. Arnold later led Loyalist troops in Virginia. After the war, Arnold lived in England, where he unhappily discovered that the British scorned him for treason just as much as the Americans he had betrayed.

BY
Brigadier-General ARNOLD,
A PROCLAMATION.

To the Officers and Soldiers of the Continental Army who have the real Interest of their Country at Heart, and who are determined to be no longer the Tools and Dupes of Congress, or of France.

HAVING reason to believe that the principles I have avowed, in my address to the public of the 7th instant, animated the greatest part of this continent, I rejoice in the opportunity I have of inviting you to join His Majesty's Arms.

His Excellency Sir *Henry Clinton* has authorized me to raise a corps of cavalry and infantry, who are to be clothed, subsisted, and paid as the other troops are in the British service, and those who bring in horses, arms, or accoutrements, are to be paid their value, or have liberty to sell them: To every non-commissioned officer and private a bounty of THREE GUINEAS will be given, and as the Commander in Chief is pleased to allow me to nominate the officers, I shall with infinite satisfaction embrace this opportunity of advancing men whose valour I have witnessed, and whose principles are favourable to an union with *Britain*, and TRUE AMERICAN LIBERTY.

The rank they obtain in the King's service will bear a proportion to their former rank, and the number of men they bring with them.

It is expected that a Lieutenant-Colonel of cavalry will bring with him, or recruit in a reasonable time, 75 men,

Major of *HORSE* - 50 men.	Lieut. Col. of *INFANTRY* - 75 men.	
Captain of ditto - - - 30	Major of ditto - - - - - - - - - 50	
Lieutenant of ditto - 15	Captain of ditto - - - - - - - - 30	
Cornet of ditto - - - 12	Lieutenant of ditto - - - - - - 15	
Serjeant of ditto - - - 6	Ensign of ditto - - - - - - - - 12	
	Serjeant of ditto - - - - - - - - 6	

N. B. Each Field Officer will have a Company.

Great as this encouragement must appear to such as have suffered every distress of want of pay, hunger and nakedness, from the neglect, contempt, and corruption of Congress, they are nothing to the motives which I expect will influence the brave and generous minds I hope to have the honour to command.

I wish to lead a chosen band of Americans to the attainment of peace, liberty, and safety (that first object in taking the field) and with them to share in the glory of rescuing our native country from the grasping hand of *France*, as well as from the ambitious and interested views of a desperate party among ourselves, who, in listening to *French* overtures, and rejecting those from *Great-Britain*, have brought the colonies to the very brink of destruction.

Friends, fellow soldiers, and citizens, arouse, and judge for yourselves,—reflect on what you have lost,—consider to what you are reduced, and by your courage repel the ruin that still threatens you.

Your country once was happy, and had the proffered peace been embraced, your last two years of misery had been spent in peace and plenty, and repairing the desolations of a quarrel that would have set the interest of *Great-Britain* and *America* in its true light, and cemented their friendship; whereas, you are now the prey of avarice, the scorn of your enemies, and the pity of your friends.

You were promised LIBERTY by the leaders of your affairs; but is there an individual in the enjoyment of it, saving your oppressors? Who among you dare speak, or write what he thinks, against the tyranny which has robbed you of your property, imprisons your persons, drags you to the field of battle, and is daily deluging your country with your blood?

You are flattered with independency as preferable to a redress of grievances, and for that shadow, instead of real felicity, are sunk into all the wretchedness of poverty by the rapacity of your own rulers. Already are you disqualified to support the pride of character they taught you to aim at, and must inevitably shortly belong to one or other of the great powers their folly and wickedness have drawn into conflict. Happy for you that you may still become the fellow-subjects of *Great-Britain*, if you nobly disdain to be the vassals of *France*.

What is *America* now but a land of widows, orphans, and beggars?—and should the parent nation cease her exertions to deliver you, what security remains to you even for the enjoyment of the consolations of that religion for which your fathers braved the ocean, the heathen, and the wilderness? Do you know that the eye which guides this pen lately saw your mean and profligate Congress at mass for the soul of a Roman Catholic in Purgatory, and participating in the rites of a Church, against whose antichristian corruptions your pious ancestors would have witnessed with their blood?

As to you who have been soldiers in the continental army, can you at this day want evidence that the funds of your country are exhausted, or that the managers have applied them to their own private uses? In either case you surely can no longer continue in their service with honour or advantage; yet you have hitherto been their supporters of that cruelty, which, with an equal indifference to your, as well as to the labour and blood of others, is devouring a country, which, from the moment you quit their colours, will be redeemed from their tyranny.

But what need of arguments to such as feel infinitely more misery than tongue can express. I therefore only add my promise of the most affectionate welcome and attention to all who are disposed to join me in the measures necessary to close the scene of our afflictions, which, intolerable as they are, must continue to increase until we have the wisdom (shewn of late by *Ireland*) in being contented with the liberality of the Parent Country, who still offers her protection, with the immediate restoration of our ancient privileges, civil ... ion from all taxes, but such as we shall think fit to impose on ourselves,

                                                                          B. ARNOLD.

British Major John André (c. 1751-80; above, left) sketched this self-portrait the day before he was hanged. André was in charge of General Henry Clinton's intelligence operations—a post that led to his fateful meeting with Arnold. Because he was caught in civilian clothing, he was hanged as a spy rather than simply being taken prisoner.

This etching (above, right) depicts General Charles Lee (1758-82) who was suspended from the army for his actions at the Battle of Monmouth. He wanted an apology from Washington, who angrily refused.

INDIANS AND THE REVOLUTION

The Indian tribes that lived around the colonies became involved in the Revolutionary War. Most tribes wished to remain neutral. "We are unwilling to join on either side of such a contest, for we love you both—old England and new," said an Oneida chief when the war began. Both the British and the Americans believed most Indians were savages and should not be involved. The British, however, had established ties with certain tribes long before the war broke out. In 1778, Washington sent a force under General George Rogers Clark against the Iroquois of western New York. A second force, led by General John Sullivan, followed a year later. Although little fighting occurred, the Americans burned the natives' villages and crops. With their food and homes destroyed, the Iroquois could not help the British.

Thayendaneken (1742-1807; above), also known as Joseph Brant, was an Iroquois chief of the Mohawk nation. Educated at the Indian School (which became Dartmouth College) in New Hampshire, Brant was made "Colonel of Indians" by the British. In the late 1770s and early 1780s he led the Iroquois on a series of devastating raids against towns on the New York frontier.

In the summer of 1777, an Iroquois war party traveling with British General John Burgoyne's army killed Jane McCrea, the wife of an American settler in New York. News of the attack traveled swiftly among the region's frontier settlements. Angered at the brutal murder, shown in this nineteenth-century illustration (opposite page, bottom), many settlers joined the American forces preparing to attack Burgoyne in the Saratoga campaign.

American General John Sullivan (1740-95, above, left) led the 1779 campaign against the British army's Iroquois and Loyalist allies, destroying their villages and crops in the Mohawk Valley.

George Rogers Clark (1751-1818; above, right), a frontiersman and military leader, began his career by surveying and clearing land in the Ohio River Valley. His victories against both the British and their Native American supporters during the Revolutionary War helped secure the frontier and open it for settlement.

THE WAR
MOVES SOUTH

In late 1778, the British launched a campaign to gain control of the southern colonies. On December 29, British forces captured Savannah, Georgia; a month later Augusta, Georgia also fell. Twice, the British attacked Charleston, South Carolina; in June 1779, they failed, but they succeeded the second time, in May 1780. The fall of Charleston, an important seaport, was a severe defeat; the British captured five thousand American troops, along with many ships and large amounts of weapons and supplies. In an attempt to reverse the British gains, the Americans—with support from the French navy and 5,500 veteran French soldiers—tried unsuccessfully to recapture Savannah in the fall of 1779.

Realizing that his outnumbered soldiers could not defeat the British in traditional battles, General Nathanael Greene, the American commander in the South, tried a new strategy. Using guerrilla forces to keep British troops in the countryside, Greene moved his own troops from place to place to keep the British off balance. The new strategy paid off with some important American victories in late 1780 and early 1781. In October 1780, frontier Patriots defeated a thousand-man Loyalist force at Kings Mountain, North Carolina. In January 1781, American General Daniel Morgan smashed Banastre Tarleton's mostly Tory troops at Cowpens, South Carolina.

Francis Marion (c.1732-95), pictured in this nineteenth-century engraving (above), won the nickname "Swamp Fox" for his talent for attacking British and Loyalist outposts while escaping capture. Operating from the swamps of South Carolina, Marion and his small band of ill-equipped Patriot guerrillas made hit-and-run raids that helped erode British morale.

During the early fall months of 1779, the Americans and their French allies tried to take back Savannah, Georgia, from the British. This French etching (above) shows the lines of trenches the attackers dug around the British-held city. When they emerged from these trenches and assaulted Savannah, however, the British defenders drove off the French and American forces in a bloody battle.

In this engraving after a painting (below), Marion and his men cross the Pee Dee River in South Carolina. Marion's elusive tactics and the wet, muddy terrain constantly frustrated the British, who preferred to fight "set-piece" battles on open ground.

LT. COL. TARLETON.

General Nathanael Greene (1742-86; left) commanded American forces in the South after 1780. At the time he replaced General Horatio Gates, much of the South was under British control. Greene, one of the Continental Army's best generals, managed to turn the situation around by 1781.

Like Francis Marion, Daniel Morgan (1736-1802) pictured (below) in an engraving from a sketch by John Trumbull, specialized in attacking British forces in the South Carolina countryside. On January 17, 1781, Morgan and his band of Virginia riflemen crushed a British force at Cowpens, South Carolina, scoring a brilliant victory.

Lieutenant Colonel Banastre Tarleton (1754-1833) is pictured (left) with his Loyalist cavalry in this 1782 engraving. Tarleton became known as "The Butcher" after the battle at Waxhaws, South Carolina, in May 1780. Tarleton defeated the Americans but massacred over a hundred survivors instead of taking them prisoner. British General Lord Cornwallis sent Tarleton to capture Francis Marion, but the "Swamp Fox" led the ruthless Tarleton on a fruitless chase through the countryside.

WINDING DOWN THE WAR: 1781

After General Nathanael Greene took command of the Continental Army in the South, the tide of the war began to turn. By the spring of 1781, Greene's army had pushed Cornwallis's British troops into North Carolina. Elsewhere in the South, British troops were bottled up in towns and cities, unable to move through the American-controlled countryside. French troops and supplies poured in to reinforce the Americans. On March 15, 1781, Greene and Cornwallis met in battle at Guilford Court House, North Carolina. The battle was a draw, but a discouraged Cornwallis took his army to the Virigina coast. Greene's force turned south, recapturing almost all of the territory captured by the British.

In New York, the British commander in chief, Sir Henry Clinton, realized that Cornwallis was in danger of being trapped by the French and American forces. Clinton ordered Cornwallis to move north. Cornwallis refused, saying that Virginia was too important to be abandoned. Clinton's fears proved true. Washington marched his men south from their positions around New York, where they joined forces with French troops commanded by Comte de Rochambeau. Meanwhile, a French fleet under Admiral de Grasse arrived in Chesapeake Bay, cutting off the British by sea. By October, Cornwallis and his army were trapped on Virginia's Yorktown peninsula. The stage was set for the last great battle of the war.

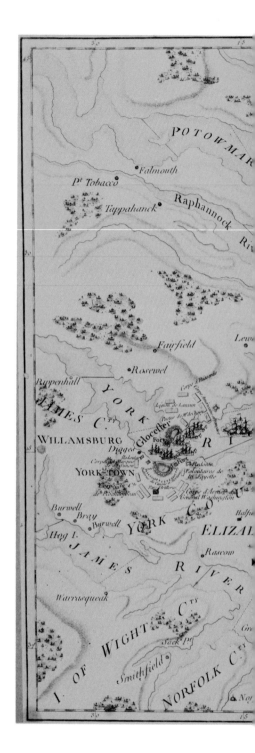

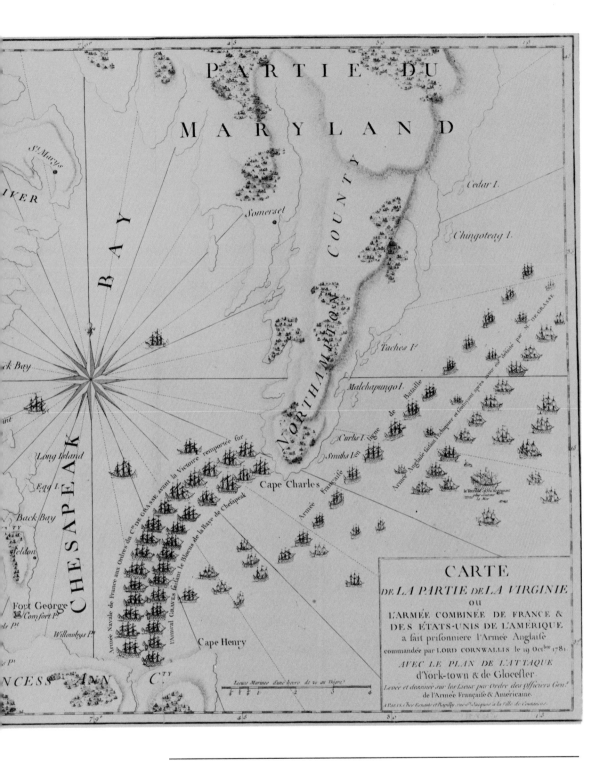

The map contains the following labels:

PARTIE DU

MARYLAND

NORTHAMPTON COUNTY

St Marys

Somerset

Cedar I.

Chingoteag I.

Taches I.

Malchapungo I.

de Bataille

Armée Angloise faisant la signne après sa défaite par M. DE GRASSE

BAY

CHESAPEAK

Long Island

Egg I.

Back Bay

Seldon

Fort George
Comfort P.

Willowbys P.

Cape Charles

Armée Françoise

Curtis I. ligne

Smiths I.en

Cape Henry

le Terrible qui sengageant
plus avant dans
la Mer

Armée Navale de France aux Ordres du cap. GRASSE avant la Victoire remportée sur l'Amiral GRAVES faisant le Blocus de la Baye de Chesapeak

NCESS ANN C.TY

Lieuë Maruee d'une heure de 20 au Degre.

CARTE

DE LA PARTIE *DE* LA VIRGINIE

OU

L'ARMÉE COMBINÉE DE FRANCE &
DES ÉTATS-UNIS DE L'AMÉRIQUE
a fait prisonniere l'Armée Angloise
commandée par LORD CORNWALLIS le 19 Oct.bre 1781

AVEC LE PLAN DE L'ATTAQUE
d'York-town & de Glocester.

Levée et dessinée sur les Lieux par Ordre des officiers Gen.x
de l'Armée Françoise & Americaine.

Published in Paris in 1781, the engraved map (above) shows Admiral de Grasse's French fleet in Chesapeake Bay. In early October, a British fleet sailed from New York to attack the French warships. De Grasse forced the British from the Virginia coast in one of the most important naval battles of the war. After the Battle of Chesapeake Bay, Cornwallis could not escape or receive reinforcements.

A British cartoon (above) makes fun of the beautifully uniformed French troops under General Rochambeau. Together, the American and French forces totaled seventeen thousand, outnumbering Cornwallis's British army by more than two to one. On October 6, General Washington personally fired the first cannon at the British positions on Yorktown Heights. The siege of Yorktown had begun.

This etching (below) shows the surrender of British troops at Yorktown on October 20, 1781. The victorious French fleet led by Admiral de Grasse floats off the coast while Washington's and Rochambeau's land forces surround the town. The allied French and American troops outnumbered the British, forcing Cornwallis to surrender his entire army.

THE SURRENDER AT YORKTOWN

The siege of Yorktown lasted less than two weeks. After eleven days of shelling by Continental and French artillery, Cornwallis sent out an officer carrying a white flag to ask for a truce in order to negotiate surrender terms. Washington found the terms Cornwallis asked for insulting. (For example, Cornwallis wanted his troops to return to Britain instead of becoming prisoners.) Angrily, Washington rejected Cornwallis's terms and prepared to resume the siege. The British commander realized that his situation was hopeless and agreed to surrender under Washington's terms.

At two o'clock on the afternoon of October 19, the British soldiers slowly marched out of their positions to lay down their muskets before the American and French troops. That evening, an American officer wrote, "This is to us a most glorious day, but to the English, one of bitter disappointment." As the British surrendered, a band played a popular tune called "The World Turned Upside Down." In a way, the world had turned upside down at Yorktown. For almost the first time in history, a colonial people had fought for their freedom against great odds—and won. The American Revolution did not end at Yorktown, however, although it was the last major battle of the war. But, the British government and people, weary of this costly, unpopular war, were now ready to accept American independence.

Cornwallis and Washington signed the document of surrender (above), called "The Articles of Capitulation," on October 19, 1781. Skirmishes between British and American forces went on for two more years, especially on the frontier, but Cornwallis's surrender marked the end of the military struggle for independence.

Lord Charles Cornwallis (1738-1805; left) had been a supporter of the Patriot cause while a member of Parliament in the 1760s. Despite his defeat at Yorktown, he had a strong record in the early years of the war. After the American Revolution, Cornwallis served the British Crown as a soldier and government official in India and Ireland.

General George Washington reviews his victorious army in this nineteenth-century Currier and Ives lithograph (below). Cornwallis did not personally give his sword to Washington in the traditional gesture of surrender. Claiming "ill health," he sent his second-in-command, General Charles O'Hara, to the surrender ceremony in his place. O'Hara tried to hand his sword to General Rochambeau. But, the French general insisted it go to George Washington, commander of the "rabble" so many British officers and politicians had scorned.

THE TREATY
OF PARIS

Both Britain and the American colonies were exhausted by the war. Neither side had achieved total military victory, but both were ready for peace. With the struggle over, America faced a new challenge—negotiating a peace treaty that would assure its independence. Work on a treaty began in Paris in March 1782. In November 1782, Britain and the United States signed a preliminary peace treaty. This caused some anger in France, since that nation, the United States's ally, had not been included in the negotiations. The French government accepted the treaty only when Britain and America promised that it would not go into effect until France also made peace with Britain. Over the next few months, America's chief diplomats— Benjamin Franklin, Henry Laurens, and John Jay—worked with British and French diplomats to draft a treaty that would be acceptable to all the nations involved. These included Holland and Spain, neither of which was an official ally of America.

The most important question to be settled was how much territory the new United States would gain. Britain, hoping to reduce French influence over America, offered to give all its North American territory (except Canada) to the United States. On September 3, 1783, the Treaty of Paris was signed. Besides settling boundaries, Britain pledged to respect American independence. The Continental Congress ratified the treaty on January 14, 1784.

The last British troops left New York City in December 1783. In the Currier and Ives lithograph (above), General George Washington and his army reenter New York City, greeted by cheering crowds. The Continental Army had been driven from the city in November 1776. Now, some of the same soldiers who had retreated across the Hudson more than seven years earlier marched victoriously through the city's streets.

A
MAP
of the
UNITED STATES
— of —
AMERICA,
As settled by the Peace of
1783.

Publish'd Dec.ʳ,1783,by I.Fielding,Pater-noster Row.

The map (above) shows the territory of the United States of America as settled by the Treaty of Paris in 1783. Besides the thirteen original colonies, now called states, the new nation included the vast wilderness stretching west from the Appalachian Mountains to the Mississippi River. During the peace negotiations, Benjamin Franklin had suggested that Britain also give Canada to the United States to prevent "future difficulties." However, the British kept Canada. Despite the generous terms of the treaty, Britain illegally maintained a few military outposts in the territory won by America.

In this famous painting by John Trumbull (below) General George Washington resigns his commission before the Continental Congress at Annapolis, Maryland. Days earlier, Washington had bid farewell to the Continental Army officers at Fraunces Tavern in New York City. With the war over, Washington returned to Mount Vernon, his Virginia plantation. He hoped to spend the rest of his life as a gentleman farmer, but it would not be long before the new nation would need his leadership and wisdom once again.

This nineteenth-century illustration (above) shows Continental Army soldiers returning home after the long struggle for independence. The Continental Army's troubles did not end at Yorktown. Lack of pay and supplies (some troops had not been paid in years) led to mutinies in a few units. Many officers were angered by the Continental Congress's neglect of their men's needs. One group of officers secretly proposed to overthrow Congress and make Washington a military dictator. Washington heard of the plot and angrily quashed it. He had not fought long and hard for freedom, he said, for the new nation to fall into tyranny.

A committee appointed by the Continental Congress began working on a design for the official Seal of the United States of America on July 4, 1776. This sketch (right) of an eagle with thirteen stars above its head representing the thirteen states was adopted as the new nation's seal on June 20, 1782.

As this British cartoon (below) states, America had indeed triumphed. Many people in Britain had expected the "rebellion" to be put down quickly when fighting began in April 1775. Instead, an army of sixty thousand men had failed to crush the movement for independence. The American Revolution shook the British government to its foundations. George III was so angered by the British defeat at Yorktown that he offered to give up his crown.

Resource Guide

Key to picture positions: (T) top, (C) center, (B) bottom; and in combinations: (TL) top left, (TC) top center, (TR) top right, (BL) bottom left, (BC) bottom center, (BR) bottom right, (CR) center right, (CL) center left.

Key to picture locations within the Library of Congress collections (and where available, photo negative numbers): P - Prints and Photographs; HABS - Historical American Buildings Survey (div. of Prints and Photographs); R - Rare Book Division; G - General Collections; MSS - Manuscript Division; G&M - Geography and Map Division.

PICTURES IN THIS VOLUME

2-3 Evacuation, P, USZ62-45548 6-7 Washington, P 8-9 map, G 10-11 title page, P, USZ62-50794.

Timeline I:
12 TL, Burke, G; TR, North, P, USZ62-45503; B, Minutemen, P 13 T, George III, P, USZ62-21623; BL, Washington, P, USZ62- 45181; TR, flag, G 14 T, steam engine, G; BL, Paine, P, USZ62-8238; BC, evacuation, P; BR, Cornwallis, P, USZ62-45340 15 T, Hume, G; BL, signing, P, USZ62-820; BR, British, P, USZ62-26673 16-17 TL, Resolution, P, USZ62-39573; TR, Lexington, P, USZ62-39582; BR, map, G&M 18-19 TL, Concord, P, USZ62-5543; TR, title page, P, USZ62-77324 20-21 TL, Knox, P, USZ62-45244; BL, forts, P; TR, Ticonderoga, G; BR, camp, P, USZ62-53576 22-23 TL, Gage, P, USZ62-45419; BL, Warren, P, USZ62-27694; TR, map, G&M; BR, Bunker Hill, P, USZ62-8624 24-25 TL, Address, MSS; TR, Battle, P, USZ62-25962; BR, poster, P 26-27 TR, document, MSS; BR, State House, P, USZ62-9486 28-29 TL, army, P, USZ62-23040; BL, poster, P, USZ62-56874; TR, Manual, P, USZ62-49633 30-31 TL, Dickinson, P, USZ62-26777; TR, Washington, P, USZ62-3620 32-33 TL, Carleton, P, USZ62-7845; TR, Arnold, P, USZ62-39570; BR, Quebec, P, USZ62-45579 34-35 TL, Falmouth, P, USZ62-45238; BL, Artillery, P, USZ62-10876; TR, ships, P, USZ62-49368 36-37 TL, Clinton, P, USZ62-45262; C, Ft. Sullivan, G&M; TR, hairdo, P, USZ62-46309 38-39 Statue, P, USZ62-22023.

Timeline II:
40 T, Louis XVI, G; BL, reading, P, USZ62-11336; BR, Hale, P 41 TL, Charles III, G; TC, Gibbon, G; TR, Mozart, G; BL, fire, P, USZ62-42; BR, Cornwallis, P, USZ62-39563 42 TL, Lavoisier, G; BL, Princeton, P, D416-698; BC, Arnold, P, USZ62-39570; BR, Lafayette, P, USZ62-45525 43 T, Cook, G; BL, Howe, P, USZ62-45179; BR, surrender, P, USZ62-39585 44-45 TL, Hancock, P, USZ62-45235; TR, Lee, P, USZ62-7680; BR, Committee, P 46-47 TL, Jefferson, G; BL, draft, P, USP6-187Λ-191Λ; TR, Declaration, P,

USZ62-11336 48-49 TL, public reading, G; TR, Franklin's plan, MSS; BR, Articles, P, USZ62-59464 50-51 TL, meeting, P, USZ62-50793; TR, cartoon, P, USZ62-8356; BR, mob scene, P, USZ62-51681 52-53 TL, drawing, G&M; TR, Howe, P, USZ62-45179; BR, list, G&M 54-55 Troops, P, USZ62-26673 56-57 TL, Hessians, P, USZ62-19419; C, Delaware, P; TR, Wayne, P, USZ62-45242; BR, map, G&M 58-59 TL, Gates, P, USZ62-45258; BL, British camp, P, USZ62-31881; C, Lincoln, P, USZ62-45245; TR, Burgoyne, P, USZ62-45354; BR, surrender, P, USZ62-39585 60-61 TL, von Steuben, P, USZ62-45483; BR, Valley Forge, P, USZ62-57 62-63 Franklin's reception, P, USZ62-19420.

Timeline III:
64 TL, Voltaire, G; TR, warship, P, USZ62-112; BL, Clinton, P, USZ62-45262; BC, Articles, P, USZ62-59464; BR, Jones, P, USZ62-45184 65 B, Adams, P, USZ62-1798 66 T, Hastings, G; B, Yorktown, P, USZ62-22034 67 T, Marie Antoinette, G; BL, cartoon, P, USZ62-1540; BR, Treaty, G 68-69 TL, Franklin, P, USZ62-1434; TR, Vergennes, P, USZ62-45183; BR, cartoon, P, USZ62-46427 70-71 TL, allegory, P, USZ62-29192; TR, Lafayette, P, USZ62-820; BR, ships, P, USZ62-900 72-73 TL, Jones, P, USZ62-45184; BR, ships, P, USZ62-112 74-75 TL, West Point, G&M; C, Major Andre, P, USZ62-68989; TR, Charles Lee, G; BR, broadside, MSS 76-77 TL, Thayendaneken, P, USZ62-45500; C, Sullivan, P, USZ62-39567; TR, Clark, P, USZ61-140; BR, attack, G 78-79 BL, camps, P, USZ62-11898; TR, Marion, P, USZ61-71; BR, river, P, USZ62-8348 80-81 TL, Tarleton, P, USZ62-48487; TR, Greene, P, USZ62-45507; BR, Morgan, P, USZ62-16371 82-83 C, map, G&M 84-85 TL, French Army, P, USZ62-1518; C, battle, G&M 86-87 TL, document, MSS; TR, Cornwallis, P, USZ62-45340; BR, Washington, P 88-89 TL, reception, P; TR, map of U.S., R 90-91 C, Washington resigning, P, USA7-12759; TR, army, P, 92-93 TL, cartoon, P; TR, Arms of U.S., P, USZ62-45508.

SUGGESTED READING

MCPHILLIPS, MARTIN. *The Battle of Trenton.* New York: Silver Burdett, 1986.

RUSSEL, FRANCIS. *Lexington, Concord and Bunker Hill.* Mahwah, NJ: Troll Associates, 1963.

CUNLIFFE, MARCUS. *George Washington and the Making of a Nation.* Mahwah, NJ: Troll Associates, 1966.

SMITH, CARTER. *Colonial and Revolutionary America.* New York: Facts on File, 1990.

MORRISON, SAMUEL E. *The Oxford History of the American People.* New York: Oxford University Press, 1965.

The American Heritage Illustrated History of the United States, volume 3. New York: American Heritage, 1988.

The Life History of the United States, volumes 1, 2, 3. Alexandria, Virginia, 1977.

ENCYCLOPEDIA BRITTANICA. *The Annals of America,* volume 2. Chicago: Encyclopedia Brittanica Inc.,

Index

Page numbers in *italics* indicate illustrations.